Sabrina Fox

Loved by Angels

Angels are right beside us— even if we don't yet see them

Sabrina Fox

Loved by Angels

Angels are right beside us—
even if we don't yet see them

Bluestar
Communications®
Woodside, California

Translation by Sabrina Fox

First Published in German by
Droemersche Verlagsanstalt Th. Knaur Nachf., Munich, Germany
under the title
Wie Engel uns lieben
© 1997 Droemersche Verlagsanstalt Th. Knaur Nachf., Munich, Germany

This Translation
© 1999 Bluestar Communications
44 Bear Glenn
Woodside, CA 94062
Tel: 800-6-Bluestar

Edited by Jude Berman

Cover Art by Edward Hughes
Night with her Train of Stars by Edward Hughes
With Courtesy of Birmingham Museum and Art Gallery, Birmingham, England
Photograph on Page 272   © Claudette Barius

Cover design: Petra Michel
Layout: Petra Michel

First printing 1999

ISBN: 1-885394-32-2

Library of Congress Cataloging-in-Publication Data
Fox, Sabrina, 1958-
    [Wie Engel uns lieben.   English]
    Loved by angels : how to meet your guardian angel / Sabrina Fox.
        p. cm.
    ISBN 1-885394-32-2
    1. Guardian angels.   I. Title.
    BT966.2.F6913   1998
291.2'15--dc21   98-16736
                                                                        CIP

Printed in USA

To God,
without whose love
I would not exist
and to
Julia and Richard—
You are my blessings.

In loving memory
of
Jacqueline Snyder

Contents

Chapter Seventeen

Acknowledgments

All those experiences that came as blessings to me would not have been possible without those sisters and brothers that were sent my way and who shared a part of my life with me. To honor each and everyone of them in an appropriate way would fill this book by itself.

From the bottom of my heart, I would like to thank my family, my Sacred Life family, my sisters in-spirit, the friends of The Country School, the wonderful angels from Bluestar Communications, my friends who have wondered at times but stayed with me throughout all my changes.

Deeply and with great humility, I give thanks
to the wisdom and love of Jesus Christ,
to my beloved Zarathustra,
and to all my heavenly messengers
and Liquid Blue.

**If you wish to know whether you should read this book,
just hold it to your heart
and ask your Angel to send you a feeling.
One day, we will all learn to follow our hearts.**

Preface

Miracles have become a part of my life since I connected with my Angels.

Last January, my sister-in-spirit Sharon Walker came to visit me in my home in Los Angeles. While in my sanctuary, she looked at a painting she had once painted for me and said: "Oh it's time now!" I stared at the painting—it was a painting showing me from the side, completely immersed in blue waves and there was a single white star in the upper left corner—but I had no clue what she meant. "Time for what?" I asked. "You need to have a blue star in your painting. I saw it in my dream. I am going to paint it tomorrow."—"Why?" I asked. She just smiled.

Three months later I became very restless. For more than six months my German publisher had tried to find an American publishing house for the English edition of my book, without success. It seemed that I had to learn patience, once again. I am usually a 'get the job done' kind of person but every time my mind tells me to do something to speed up this process, my spirit says "no."

I live in the United States now, but having been a German television host for many years I published "Loved by Angels" in Germany first; it just seemed to be the right choice. However, I always felt my angel book would eventually be published in English as well … but nothing was happening. Was I wrong? I placed my faith in God's hands and waited, but … was he doing anything? Sometimes God's timing was not my timing and I wanted an answer so badly. I longed for a message similar to: "Yes, it will be published, just wait a day … a month … a year … a century." I needed that answer. It is so much easier to be patient when you know exactly how long you must wait ….

I had asked my angels for an answer. Over the past four years I have learned how to ask such questions and I will be sharing this experience and technique with you in my book. But I had not received any answer. So early in March, it was the second, a Monday, I couldn't wait any longer. I wanted at least a sign, but a clear one. Not one I could fiddle around with, no, I wanted a clear sign. I meditated in the morning and for one hour I just held one thought: "Beloved Heavenly Father, I pray to Thee for a sign within the next twenty four hours, whether or not my book will ever be published in English."

After I had finished my meditation, I returned to my desk and began to answer a letter. Ten minutes later the fax machine rang. I glanced over to see that it was my German publishing house sending me a fax: "We have a publisher. The name: Bluestar!" I was stunned. I love miracles! I fell on my knees and thanked God. I couldn't get a clearer sign. Once again, I knew everything was part of a divine plan.

Life becomes easier when we follow God. In the past, I used to go ahead with my own plan no matter what. That wasn't working at all. I was one of those people who tries to impress the world with her intelligence but deep down I felt very vulnerable and, therefore, tried hard to develop a thicker skin. However, this didn't work either and instead I developed a good degree of cynicism.

When my life as a successful television host fell apart, when my shows were cancelled, I lost my identity. I only felt valuable while society accepted me, preferably even envied me. When all that vanished, I lost "my self"—or better, I lost what I thought *was* my self. After these events I looked for help in spirituality. However, even then I had only one goal in my mind: How could I possibly change the people around me and/or find new acquaintances who would better suit my own needs? For I believed at that time that I myself was perfectly okay and only the others were the problem: *their* attitudes, *their* actions, *their* reactions. After I had spent some time seriously thinking about God, soul, reincarnation and choice, a different thought crept up within me, a thought I didn't really like at first: "Maybe, just maybe, *I* have to change."

Then God sent His angels to help me. If you think about it, that was quite a smart thing to do, because I never had a close relationship with God Himself—not that I had any relationship with angels either at that time. Back then, I thought angels only existed in fairy tales and Bible stories, or on wonderfully decorated Christmas trees. So, one day my dear friend Rita began telling me about those heavenly messengers. That's how angels found their way into my heart. From that time on, my angels encouraged me to see the bigger picture. Through them, I realized that life actually makes quite a lot of sense! That was a totally new approach for me.

When we have angels in our lives, our minds and hearts open and we are reminded of how life was originally in-

tended to be: glorious, exciting, happy and joyful. The feeling of loneliness leaves us. We belong! Through our dreams and visions, we can create a new life that is completely different from the "old" life we knew so well. We no longer have the overwhelming feeling of exhaustion, of being victimized by outer circumstances over which we have no control, or the experience of ending one crisis just to find out it is being followed by another.

I wrote this book to share with you the joy of a life in God; the excitement, the choices, the care and—as far as I know—the wisdom of it. In this book, I share true angel experiences with you, my friends' experiences as well as my own. Theirs are experiences of proof, while mine are of faith, because I have not yet seen angels.

"Do angels really exist", I was asked once and I answered: "Of course they do. Look at all the Holy Scriptures; every religion, every faith, every indigenous culture knows about angels or 'winged ones.' Why should we assume they are not here anymore? Do you think they have taken a vacation? For 2000 years?"

They *are* here—even if we don't yet see them! To feel them, just close your eyes, pray, sing, ask, or just turn the next page …

Sabrina Fox
Los Angeles, May 1998

Chapter One

About an Angel in my bedroom and the question why some Angels can be seen

Esther, our housekeeper, was somehow different from normal. I noticed a spark in her brown eyes I hadn't seen before, and she hugged me longer and squeezed me tighter than usual before letting me go. "Is everything all right?" I asked her.

"Everything is perfectly all right," she answered. "Welcome home."

My husband Richard, our daughter Julia and I had just come back from a long weekend in Santa Barbara, where we had celebrated my husband's birthday. While we were away, Esther had stayed at our home, as she usually does, to care for our dog Sister and our cats Barney, Boots and Greyfur.

We live off Benedict Canyon, in Los Angeles. In the canyon, our neighbors are coyote, deer and hawks, as well as spiders, mice and many ants. When you fly over the Los Angeles area and see the vast urban sprawl, you would not expect to encounter such diversity of wildlife. Having spent most of my life in Bavaria, Germany, the only animals I miss here are the cows. Whenever we return home, one of my first questions to Esther is always: "Where is so and so?" depending on which animal hasn't come out to greet us. I ask this especially since I have observed that coyotes love to have cat for dessert.

When we arrived home from Santa Barbara, Julia ran to play with Esther's daughter, Roxana, my husband went into

the living room to check the mail and Esther and I went into the bedroom to unpack the bags. "What's up?" I asked Esther as I removed the stones I had collected on the beach from my duffel bag. Esther did not reply. Thinking maybe she hadn't heard me, I asked again, "Esther?"

She stared absentmindedly at the red cloth wrapped around my travel altar. "Is everything all right?" I asked again.

"I saw your guardian angel!" she whispered.

"My guardian angel?" I was astonished. "Tell me about it." I sat down on the bed and looked up at Esther. She was playing nervously with her beautiful brown curls.

"Exactly where you are sitting is where I saw her," she said, pointing her finger at me.

"Okay. Let's start from the beginning. When and where did you see this angel?"

Her whole face lit up as she began the story: "Right after you left, I changed the linen on the beds. Then Roxanna and I walked the dog. When we came back around 8 p.m., we had dinner. My husband picked up Roxanna and shortly after that I got very tired and decided to go to bed. I lay on your side of the bed and fell asleep almost immediately."

She took a deep breath, then continued: "In the middle of the night, I felt something come into my body. I've never felt anything like that in my life! It was not a dream. It was real. I got quite hot and someone deep inside of me moved my body. As I woke up, I noticed my left arm move by itself."

"Move by itself?" I asked with surprise. "How did your arm move?"

She searched for words to describe the movement while moving her arm in a wavy motion. As I watched her hand, it dawned on me: "It looks like you're waving at some-one."

"That's right," she said. "I remember clearly thinking, 'For heaven's sake, what is this?' Then I prayed the Lord's Prayer. I focused on the prayer so I could forget the experi-ence I'd just had. And I moved to the middle of the bed because your side was a little too scary for me."

"Why was that?"

Esther looked at me mischievously. "What do I know about what you experience every night? I mean, you have your meditation room; you're a hypnotherapist; you own a sacred pipe. Maybe what I felt would be normal for you."

I had to laugh. It's true I've had some extraordinary ex-periences in my life. But unfortunately not every night.

"Somehow, I fell asleep again," she continued, her gaze far in the distance. "But I woke up again because my arm began to move. As I opened my eyes, I had the sense that whatever was in me moved forward and materialized in front of me. I saw colors form into the most beautiful figure." She smiled and showed me her arm. "Look! Just talking about it gives me goose bumps."

"What colors did you see?"

"They went from violet to purple, then to strong pink. They were all from the same color group." She paused, then added, "She had a beautiful face and she smiled at me."

"She?"

"Yes." Esther folded her hands. "The angel was definitely female."

"Did you see her face clearly? Did you see hair or wings?"

"No," she replied. "It wasn't like that. The colors became the angel's form. She was lighter on the periphery, and she moved within herself, a little like water or clouds would move."

"What happened next?" I wanted to know.

"I started to pray again. I said to the angel, 'I'm not Sabrina. Sabrina is on vacation.'"

I laughed aloud. "Esther, this was *your* guardian angel, not mine! Angels know if we're at home or not."

"Yes, I thought about that, too." She joined in my laughter. "Imagine my predicament, Sabrina. There I was in your house, in your bedroom, in your bed! So I thought, this angel must be yours. She probably comes all the time and you just haven't mentioned her to me."

"I wish that were the case," I said with a smile. "Did the angel do anything?"

"The angel stayed while I was praying. Then I thought, 'Maybe this is a soul who doesn't know where she belongs.' What do I know? So I prayed just in case, 'Dear God, if this soul does not know where she belongs, please help her find the way. In the name of the Father, the Son and the Holy Spirit.' After I had finished my prayer, I looked at the angel. But she didn't look lost. She was very quiet and very sweet. After awhile she slowly disappeared."

"Did you fall asleep again?"

"Not for the longest time. There were so many questions in my mind: Who was that? Why did she come? Why did she come to me? Was this an angel looking for you? I looked out the window and prayed morning would come."

"Why did you do that?"

"The night was already too long for me. I was a little nervous about what else might happen."

"You mean, one angel was enough for one night?"

"Exactly." Esther sighed.

It was unusually quiet in the bedroom. Neither of us moved. We just smiled at one another. "That was wonderful," I heard myself say.

"You know what was interesting about it?" she asked.

I shook my head.

"Before I had this experience with my angel, whenever I was angry or sad, I was only angry or sad."

"I don't understand."

"It's difficult to explain. The angel gave me a gift. It was a wonderful feeling of love. Now when I am angry or sad, I know I can always connect with this feeling of love. My sadness is not so deep anymore and my anger is not so big. There is more in my life now; there is someone who watches over me. I have seen my guardian angel."

I stood up and hugged her. We embraced for awhile. I was so happy for her. "Did you tell the girls?" I asked finally.

"No, no," she answered quickly. "I wanted to talk with you first."

Often people tell children about angels and fairies, at least as long as they appear in fairy tales or in the Bible, but they are quiet when they have real angel experiences. I work as a spiritual counselor and a public speaker and my clients frequently ask, "How can I help my children embrace their spirituality?" When I ask them if they share their own experiences, they say, "Oh no, they wouldn't understand that." Children understand more than we do. They have not been here on earth long enough to have forgotten about God.

I opened the bedroom window and yelled, "Julia, Roxana, please come in!"

A few minutes later Roxana and Julia were sitting breathless on my bed. "Esther has seen an angel in our bedroom," I said.

"Is she still here?" Julia looked around.

"What did she look like?" Roxana wanted to know. As Esther began to explain, I left the three alone. I was thrilled we could share such a wonderful experience with our children. My daughter was six and Roxana was eleven. Since children watch very closely what their parents do, the best way to teach is by example. I am confident that when our children have their own angel experiences they will feel free to talk openly about it because it was part of their life from an early age.

As I walked into the kitchen, I felt happy but also a bit frustrated and impatient because I only see angels in my meditations. I wondered: Why have I never seen an angel in "real" life, when I am awake, with my eyes open? What am I doing wrong? Am I not ready yet? Why can Esther see her angel, and I can't? Why do angels come to one and not another? Esther hadn't even asked to see an angel while I prayed daily about it. Could her angel hear better than mine? I was very happy about Esther's experience, but I wished it would happen to me, too. Was my wish not strong enough? My desire was so intense I felt a slight pain in my heart.

The feeling of frustration and sadness did not go away. I knew I should take care of unpacking, looking through my mail and buying the groceries. But I had learned over the years that it is as important to take care of my soul as it is to manage my daily routine. Almost automatically I found myself in the back yard sitting under one of my favorite trees, a chestnut. Under the tree is a little bench and next to it is a large shovel. Still frustrated, I picked up the shovel and began to dig up the earth. Our body comes from the earth, our food comes from the earth and our medicine comes from the earth. For this reason, I felt a need to put my feet deep in the earth. I could use a little healing. I looked up at the tree. It was tall and so its roots must be deep roots, otherwise it would fall. The tree, I thought, is just like us: we must have both feet in the ground so our souls can fly even higher.

I remember, years ago I felt my body was the prison of my soul. I wanted to spend as much time as possible out of it. My deepest wish was to just meditate and leave the ordinary life behind. I couldn't wait to have only spiritual people around me, who knew exactly what I meant when I spoke of chakras, energy fields and past lives. I was very close to becoming spiritually arrogant. What can I say? I *was* spiritually arrogant!

Feeling this way hindered my spiritual development. I felt comfortable in my meditations and uncomfortable in my daily life. It took some time before I understood it was my job to be spiritual in all aspects of life—inside my body, as well as outside. Of course, we would all be saints within a week if we could live on top of a mountain with two other saints. But this is not the challenge. The challenge is to be a saint even if there are no other saints around.

At that time, I noticed that all my wishes were in my meditations and dreams but none manifested in my life. I wondered why. Am I not meditating enough?—The opposite was true. They all got stuck somewhere in-between because I didn't have a good relationship with my body or the earth. So I started to work with Native American wisdom, and with some wise women who taught me to live in balance with nature. I learned to see my body as my temple and to take care of it. I made a habit of honoring nature and staying in close contact with it. Before, I never walked barefoot on the earth because I was afraid I would hurt myself—

besides, I didn't want to have dirty feet. As I learned more about nature, I decided my perfect nails weren't as important as my curiosity and determination to learn something new.

22

As I sink my feet deep within the earth and sense the moisture on my skin, I feel the power that comes through the soil into my body.

Chapter Two

About my Angels Lucas, Euphenia and Jao and why Ivan is not always Ivan the Terrible

Sitting under the chestnut tree in our backyard, I closed my eyes and allowed the feeling of frustration to take over. I searched for the center of this feeling. As I scanned my body, I noticed the frustration was a heaviness that laid on my chest. How large was this heaviness? I searched for the end of it and sensed it extended down into my navel. It pulsated slowly and with difficulty. My frustration was a knot in my stomach.

I knew the prayer that would get me out of this feeling: "In the light of the Creator where highest truth resides and vibrates, I welcome these frequencies in the field of the domain I occupy on earth. May it be received into my psyche as wisdom beyond all wisdom that the glory that comes to me in teaching be understood and comprehended by the highest by which it is brought to me. May all the others who are of a lesser understanding fall by the wayside to follow the wind. For I shall soar to the highest from the highest within me. The most direct and swiftest route I pledge myself to. Amen."

I breathed in and out for awhile and repeated my prayer until the heaviness in my chest became lighter and eventually disappeared completely. A warmth came over me in waves and I imagined myself under a large rainbow. I focused on the different colors of the rainbow and asked one color after another to come into my body for healing. Shortly thereafter I found myself standing on top of a mountain with my arms outstretched. I heard myself yell, "My angels where are you? I want to see you!"

I heard some very high sounds and voices that said, "We are always here."

I looked around for Jao, one of my angels who has been working with me a lot lately. He is a young man who has many colors around him. Even though I know he is smiling, I can't see him very clearly with my inner eye.

"Jao," I asked. "Why can't I see you?"

I heard his answer after a short while in my head: "Do you want to see me to have a confirmation?"

I was quiet, listening. Did I need confirmation? Perhaps not. I had no doubt angels exist. I just wished to have the experience of seeing an angel, to find the connection between their invisible world and my human visible world. Tears came to my eyes. No, that was not the truth. My angels were right: I wanted confirmation.

A feeling of love swept over me and I knew that, as always, my angels were sending it to me. I felt so small, without trust or wisdom. I yelled at myself, "Why can't you just stop this wish for confirmation? This is probably why you don't see with your own eyes the things you want to see." I took a deep breath and decided not to think that thought again. I would think about something else, something that showed how much I had learned.

"Don't you remember?" asked Jao. "A short time ago you were full of fears and worries."

Yes, that was true. With my inner eye I could see myself one evening four years ago, in a hotel in Hamburg, Germany. I sat on the hotel bed, exhausted and tired, with no

tears left. I had just finished taping a television show when I was told that this would be the last one because the show had been canceled. For me, it was like a death sentence.

The clothes I had worn during the taping were thrown over a chair, my hair was still moist from the shower and my T-shirt was wet from my tears. My career was finished, or so I felt. My very existence was threatened. For ten years, being in front of a camera on television had been my life. Although I had gotten married to a wonderful man four years earlier, moved to Los Angeles, given birth to a wonderful and healthy daughter, lived in a great house and had a nice set of friends, I was more "me" on television than at home.

My career was my confirmation that I had made it. I, Sabrina, who had been thrown out of my home at age seventeen by an alcoholic father, who at that time had not even finished high school, was broke and sixty pounds overweight, had nevertheless set out to conquer the world. And that's what I had done until I lost everything all over again, including my self-esteem.

In my head the pictures began to flash even faster. I remembered Rita, my girlfriend who introduced me to spirituality. "Look how much more you understand now than back then," the images in my head seemed to say. It was true. I had learned to meditate and how to use my hands to send love and energy. I had studied hypnosis and become a hypnotherapist. Now I spent days praying in the mountains and conducted workshops and seminars about spiritual development. I was a pipe carrier. I wrote books and magazine articles and gave talks about God, angels and universal law. I was calm and without worries. None of this had I known about four years ago.

"No," Jao reminded me. "You knew, you just forgot."

Thank you. Yes, I just have to remember. We all just have to remember. How important is it really that I see my angels? Is it not enough that I can hear and feel them? I know they exist. Haven't I received confirmation many, many times? I went even deeper into meditation, to a state where time no longer exists.

Each of us has many angels. I learned that awhile ago. My first angel was introduced to me during a spiritual workshop by the facilitator, who told me my angel is called Lucas. The name was given to me, yet I never had a real relationship with Lucas. Once in meditation, I saw a huge nose and once a couple of closed eyes. But that was it.

For weeks and weeks after that, I continued to meditate … but nothing happend … until in meditation a few months later I saw a huge white body that looked like it was composed of clouds and heard the name Euphenia. A female angel with a funny name, I thought. She moved closer to me and hugged me and all of a sudden I felt peace and comfort inside. I knew I was loved unconditionally. I felt deep trust and devotion. I absorbed this feeling like a person craving water in the desert.

I asked Euphenia why she had come, and she told me she had come to assist me in using my talents.

"Which talents?" I asked.

"The talent to give the people around you understanding for themselves and each other. You will bring them together through communication and creativity." Back then I had no clue what she meant. But I have come to do exactly that.

Then there was Ivan. This angel came to me like a flood over dry land.

One morning I was on the phone discussing with my travel

agent plans for a visit from my mother and Aunt Erna. Absolutely everything was going wrong. Frustrated, I decided to take some time and meditate. I lit a candle, burned some sage and said my prayer. Then I lay flat on the floor to meditate. But my thoughts were running around like a storm in my head. The only thing I could focus on was my anger over the incompetence of the travel agent and the airline.

Suddenly I saw a huge person falling toward me. Just in the last second he caught himself with the palms of his hands directly on top of me. This huge man looked like a genie out of a bottle, with massive muscles rippling everywhere. In a huge voice, he yelled at me, "Drop it!"

I immediately stopped thinking about the incompetence of my travel agent and stared at him with my inner eye. If this were an angel, I thought, they must have body building clubs on the other side! He was huge; compared to me, he was as big as a ten-story house. He wore wide, Arabic-looking pants and his muscled chest was barely covered by a short vest.

"I'm Ivan," he stated, standing in front of me, his arms crossed over his chest. I looked up. Immediately I thought of the historic figure, Ivan The Terrible. "You're supposed to be an angel?" I questioned.

Ivan looked down at me as an adult would look down at a tiny insect. "You bet I am. In the next ten weeks," he continued, "I will teach you. I will visit you every Sunday and give you your new assignment. This week I will teach you not to defend yourself. Never. You will learn to accept other people's opinions and to stay with yours even if nobody agrees. You will learn to trust yourself under all circumstances and to believe your truth regardless of whether the rest of the world disagrees. If someone attacks you, your opinion or your position, you will not get angry or upset, but just listen and not defend yourself. Do you understand?"

I nodded silently, then asked, "You say I am not allowed to defend myself. But I'm not going to get robbed, am I?"

Ivan looked down at me sternly. "How wonderful. Now we have two lessons this week. Defenselessness and trust." And then he was gone. I opened my eyes and wondered: What was that?

Life can be quite exciting when you do not defend yourself.

I knew a woman who treated me like a murderer because I let my cats run around outside in the canyon. She wouldn't accept that I believe it is unnatural to lock up a cat in an apartment if you have a garden. Nor would she accept that I'd rather have a happy cat who followed her natural instincts than one who was penned up inside. It was hard for me to say to this woman, "I understand your concern. You must love cats very much." Instead I bit my tongue and reminded myself she was really concerned about cats—it was just that she believed problems could be avoided by locking them up. That was her opinion, not mine. I reminded myself: Don't defend. Just accept.

After a whole week of working on my defenselessness, it got easier. My understanding for other people increased. I was no longer looking for ways to change their minds. Instead I accepted their opinions and tried to understand their reasoning. I began to be curious about what would happen the next week.

During the second week Ivan taught me to have complete control over my thoughts. He instructed me not to gossip and not to make judgments. For example, twenty minutes after my meditation, a neighbor came to my house to tell me about another person we both know. Because I was curious to hear what she had to say, I tried to convince myself: This is not gossip, this is information.

"Stop it," I heard myself say in my mind.

"I would stop, but my neighbor is talking!" I tried to excuse myself.

"Interrupt her."

Okay, I could do that. "Barbara," I said, "to tell you the truth, I'm not really interested in that. I'd rather hear how you're doing."

Barbara stared at me. "Well, I'm all right, except for my back pain…"

I was very busy during this week. Each negative thought was sent away with the words, "I don't want you. I don't need you. Go into the light." I understood that I had to watch my thoughts very carefully, otherwise they were like a pack of untrained dogs. It was up to me to realize I have the leash in my hands and can control where they are going.

The third week Ivan gave me a star on my forehead. My job was to focus on this star at all times in order to remind myself to include my higher Self more and more in my daily life. I was surprised: This is all I have to do?

"This is plenty," Ivan assured me.

And he was right. While I was brushing my teeth, taking a shower, talking on the phone, driving my car, shopping, in the office, meditating, playing—all the time I had to imagine the star on my forehead. I noticed that many people gave me a funny look. I didn't know what they were seeing, but something was happening. I had never seen so many people smile at me.

The following week my assignment was to imagine the color blue around my body as much as possible. And in the fifth week I had to imagine that my third eye, the inner eye between my eyebrows, was wide open.

In the sixth week Ivan gave me the assignment to open my chakras as if they were huge circles, and to leave them open. In the seventh week he showed me how to control negative emotions by imagining an obelisk connecting all the chakras. When I practiced that for the first time, I was able to control my pulse rate and my tears. Not bad, Ivan.

In the eighth week I wasn't allowed to talk about myself. I could only listen. I became aware of how often I talked about myself, and how much I interrupted others so I could share my ideas and thoughts with them. "Let them finish, it's their turn!" was a sentence I repeated at least a thousand times that week.

In the ninth week Ivan smiled for the first time as he gave me my new job for the week: "Enjoy each moment!" Ah, finally something easy, I thought—until I was in bumper-to-bumper traffic. Enjoy each moment? What was there to enjoy? Well, I was sitting comfortably ... and the weather was nice ... But I really couldn't say I was enjoying each moment.

Okay, I thought, I do have a little bit of quiet time for myself here... I can smile at other drivers. Maybe then they will have less reason to get angry. I looked out the window at the guy in the next car. He was obviously upset. He looked in my direction.

I smiled.

He stopped complaining to himself and looked at me angrily.

I smiled again.

He looked away.

I was just about to give up when he looked back at me and smiled!

Wow, I thought, this is good. I'm starting to enjoy the moment.

In the tenth week I saw Ivan sitting in front of me, tenderly looking down at me. "Very well. Very well, indeed," he complimented me.

"Thank you," I answered with a smile.

"I am going to go now, but first I want to explain why you have seen me in this form."

I was curious about his answer.

"You understand strength and discipline. In this form, my muscle and height are an expression of strength and discipline. We thought you would have fun with that."

I barely understood his words and then he was gone. I wondered if that meant angels show themselves to us as we need them? Or do they have the choice to show themselves as they prefer? I thought it was wonderful Ivan had taken the trouble to change himself to teach me something. But maybe it was no trouble to change his form? Maybe it was easier than I realized.

Never before and never after have I had an angel who expected so much from me.

Then came Jao. First he called himself Jacob. He introduced himself to me after a radio interview, during which—instead of saying Lucas—I constantly referred to my first angel as Jacob. In my next meditation I wanted to find out why I had made that mistake. And there he was. He appeared as a young man dressed in colorful clothes. The first thing he said was, "I thought you would never ask!"

He taught me to trust. After awhile he changed his name to Jao. It was more of a sound than a name.

In the beginning I was always concerned when an angel

left me and a new one arrived. I thought the angel must have felt sad because I no longer cared about him anymore. That was my human way of thinking, but the angel world has a different perspective. Jealousy does not exist there. One comes when he is needed and goes when he is finished. That is how angels love us. Another flash of memory occurred.

Two years ago my angels intervened when my life was in danger. A camera crew from Germany had flown to Los Angeles to shoot a television biography about me. They stayed with me for two days and followed me around to see what I was doing and how I was doing it.

On the second day I was driving with the cameraman on a four-lane road. I was showing him all the sights of Los Angeles. "And if you look down to the right you will see between these big tall houses, the famous Hollywood sign on the hills of Hollywood," I said as we drove northbound in the left lane. And I pointed with my right hand in the direction where the houses and the Hollywood sign would show up soon.

All of a sudden I heard in my head, loud and clear, an order: "You are driving on the wrong side of the road, go to the right."

Immediately I jerked the steering wheel to the right. When I focused again on the road in front of me, I saw the frightened face of the driver who had just almost hit me.

"That was close," the cameraman said with a sigh.

I thanked my angels very much for their help. Thanks to God I hadn't questioned their commands.

"You've learned a lot in the last few years and you will continue to learn," Jao told me at the end of the meditation. I thanked them for reminding me of all the wonderful things that had happened and asked them to send me a special feeling before I left my prayer state. This feeling came from deep within my heart. It was a feeling of great comfort, of being loved and accepted. I enjoyed this feeling for awhile until I opened my eyes.

I gave thanks to the chestnut tree and the earth for this gift of healing energy during this meditation. I felt refreshed and calm.

34

Chapter Three

**About Angels that travel and
what happens when you follow the intuition of others**

Sometimes it seems as though one of us is always packing. My husband Richard and I travel so much we have the best assortment of suitcases I have ever seen. At least four to five times a year I fly to Germany for work, or to a conference or vision quest here in the States. My husband also travels somewhere in the world for business almost every other month.

This time I was packing to go to India, a country that had always fascinated me, even as a child. It was a journey I had been planning for six months. Jacqueline Snyder, visionary, author, spiritual counselor and founder of Sacred Life Ministries, had organized the trip. I was going because I wanted to spend a lot of time in silence, and in prayer and meditation. I could hardly wait. For me, these travels are like a spiritual education course. Every minute is a process of learning. Every minute is something new.

Each time I pray, I concentrate on one single thing. This time I focused on inviting all the thoughts that were important for me to decide what to take with me on this journey. Thoughts sent by my angels came to me and I had, as always, the choice of whether or not to listen to them. Of course, having done this practice for awhile, I knew the value of listening to the thoughts that came to me during and after such a prayer.

This time I saw with my inner eye the image of my little travel bag. It was clearly not the huge bag I had originally planned to take. I recalled the time I had lost a suitcase because I took it with me even after had I heard a clear "No" in my meditation. I didn't want that to happen again, so I listened to my inner voice and my angels. I trusted my intuition and packed the small bag, a little suitcase on wheels that doubled as a backpack.

I also brought with me on the airplane a little bag that holds my travel altar and my pipe. My travel altar has objects from my altar at home that want to travel with me. Before a trip, I kneel in front of my altar, close my eyes and ask which objects want to go with me. Then I pack whatever comes into my mind. For this trip, it was a feather I had found at the ocean, a stone from Germany, an angel made of crystal that my husband and daughter had given me for Mother's Day, a crystal cross and a picture of my family.

Some of my friends were staying in Rishikesh, India, at the base of the Himalayas. I wanted to spend Richard's birthday with him and, therefore, was leaving later. It was about a six-hour drive by car from Delhi, where I would be staying. As I was packing, Richard asked me. "Who will pick you up from the airport?" he asked.

"I don't know. Jacqueline said she is going to take care of it."

"How will you get from Delhi to Rishikesh?"

"I have no idea." Richard looked concerned. "When do you arrive back in Delhi?"

"Three o'clock in the morning."

"Is anyone traveling with you?" He sounded even more concerned.

"No."

My husband is a perfectionist who plans his trips down

to the last detail. He looked at me nervously. "I don't like that. I don't like that at all."

"Darling!" I jumped up and hugged him. "Don't be worried. I'm not afraid. My angels are with me."

He rolled his eyes, having heard me say that so many times. But it was obvious he was still concerned.

A few hours later, he gave me five phone numbers. "You can call them anytime when you're in India, anytime you need them," he said. "I talked to all of them and each one expects your call—even if it's at three o'clock in the morning." And he said, "I'm going to arrange for a car to pick you up."

It was a challenge to keep Richard from trying to make my arrival arrangements for me. "You don't need to do that," I assured him. "I'm not worried. Someone is going to pick me up."

"When was the last time you spoke with Jacqueline?"

I knew he was not going to be happy with my answer. "Three weeks ago."

"Three weeks?" He shook his head, and his eyes said, "I don't understand your thinking."

I understood that he couldn't understand. I had barely understood myself for a couple of years. But I had learned to trust in God and trust in my angels. Trust had replaced my fear that something terrible could happen any minute. That fear had left me slowly, like air leaking out of a balloon through a little hole. Eventually it was apparent there was nothing left but the deflated balloon, which was useless. Now I am astonished that I could once have had so much fear in my life. Years ago I was too afraid to go outside at night, or even to get the mail out of the mailbox in front of our house. Today I sleep alone in the forest.

Fear doesn't just disappear like a sock in the washing machine. Rather, fear gets smaller and smaller until at some point you don't even notice that it is not there any longer. On occasion it can come back for short moments, just long enough for you to recognize that it is fear. In such moments, I pray and connect myself with God and my angels.

I don't have any time for fear. There is so much to see, and fear is like a pair of dark glasses that stops me from seeing the light. Sometimes, however, I've noticed that fear can be a blessing. It allows me to look at those things I didn't take the time to look at. Then, once I've understood why I'm fearful, the fear leaves.

As I sat on the airplane, figuring I was going to be in the air for the next twenty-four hours, I tilted my seat back and made myself comfortable. I closed my eyes to meditate. I love to meditate on planes.

Was it time for dinner or was it breakfast? The man next to me wanted to talk, so I asked him about his plans. He was traveling to Manila on business. He told me he worked as a clothing importer, and that he was married with two children. After awhile he asked me, "And which business are you in?"

That's a good question, I thought to myself. Which kind of business am I in? "I'm in God's business," I replied with a smile.

"God's business?" I could see from his expression that he thought he had misunderstood.

I nodded.

"But you look so normal."

I had to laugh. "Yes, I do look very normal," I agreed. I explained that I write books about God, angels and spirituality, that I am a spiritual counselor and that I give counsel to the dying and facilitate workshops. He seemed curious as he listened to me.

"I have a question," he said. "In which God do you believe?"

"Is there more than one?" I asked, smiling again.

"No, I don't think so," he replied. "Are you a Hindu?"

Well, I was flying to India, after all. "Yes," I said. "I'm Hindu ... and Catholic ... and Buddhist ... and Jewish and...."

"I understand."

"For me, God is like a huge chandelier. In the middle of the chandelier is the power, the love of God, the light. Each arm of the chandelier reaches in a different direction. And each of these arms has a religion or a holy person, such as Jesus, Buddha, Zarathustra, Mohammed."

"Does God need religion?" asked my neighbor.

"No, I don't think God needs religion. But we sometimes need it. Unfortunately some religions are such that they make their members fearful so they will stay with that particular religion. But for God there is neither fear nor guilt—only experiences that bring us closer to Him." I wrapped my shawl more tightly around me. It was time to sleep. I would have to change planes soon.

It was three o'clock in the morning when we arrived in Delhi. The first thing I noticed was that the Delhi airport is not LAX. The only thing that the Delhi airport and LAX have in common is the planes. As I pulled my luggage behind me, I thanked my angels because it turned out that none of the plane's luggage had made it to Delhi. "Thank you for advising me to take my hand luggage, dear Jao," I thought as I walked past my frustrated fellow travelers.

I found my way out of the airport and stood on the curb, scanning the crowd. I was curious if I would see my name on a sign somewhere. Even though it was three o'clock in the morning, I was smiling and relaxed. I realized I was the only blond in the throng of people, but the Indian men were very respectful and no one bothered me as I stood quietly outside the terminal watching the busy airport traffic. I just stood there and waited and waited and waited.

After about thirty minutes I closed my eyes and I started to meditate—right there in the middle of the bustling airport traffic. I watched myself from above as I left my body. I rose higher and higher until I could see the whole airport and all of Delhi. I went still higher until I could see India and even higher until the whole world lay below me.

I enjoyed the quiet time up there. Then I asked my angels, "Am I going to be picked up?"

I waited for their response, knowing I didn't have to search for the answer; it would simply come to me. Suddenly I had a funny feeling, like something bubbling up from my navel to my head. The thought that came up was: "Yes."

"How much longer?" I wanted to know.

Again I waited patiently until I felt the answer bubble out of my navel: "Soon."

I thanked my angel and opened my eyes. Two minutes later a young man appeared in front of me. "Sabrina?" he asked.

"Yes." I nodded with joy.

"Wait," he said, taking my suitcase and disappearing again. As I waited, I imagined what Richard would say if he knew I was here without my suitcase and all his phone numbers. I am always happy when I recognize how much my reactions have changed. This time, as I waited by myself and watched the crowds of people, I was pleased that I was completely relaxed and worry free. I was looking forward to my adventure in India.

After some time, a dark car appeared in the midst of the hectic traffic and pulled up beside me. The window opened and the man I had met before waved at me. I climbed into the back seat. In the front seat with him was a driver who handed me a little note: "I come from Jacqueline. We bring you to Rishikesh. It takes about six hours."

I tried to hold a conversation with the gentleman but soon discovered why he had given me the piece of paper: he barely spoke any English. So I made myself comfortable for the six-hour drive to Rishikesh.

Looking out the window, I observed how the people in India drive. They blow their horns constantly. The horn is their number one means of communication:

Honk, Honk: here I am.

Honk, Honk: I want to pass by.

Honk, Honk: I pass you right now.

Honk, Honk: You want to catch me?

We made a sharp right turn onto a narrow street. Hmm, I thought, this can't be the road to Rishikesh? The next street we drove down was even narrower. It was about 4:30 in the morning and Delhi was asleep, especially this part of town. Again the car took an even smaller road. Still, I was completely calm. I had no thought such as "Oh, my God, what do I do? Here I am, in Delhi with two men I've never seen before. My luggage is in the trunk and no one knows where I am. What if—?"

Years ago I would have sat in the back seat with my nail file just to make sure I had a way to defend myself. Don't laugh. I did that once in Hungary fifteen years ago when my cab driver got lost. I was ready to defend my life or my honor, depending which was endangered first. As this memory came to mind, I suddenly laughed aloud. My two companions looked back in surprise, wondering what had struck me as funny. I simply nodded, and they did the same.

We drove up in front of a large wall. The car stopped in the yard and both my male companions left the car. I looked around. I could see a temple and several buildings so I concluded that this must be Swami Chidanand Saraswati's New Delhi ashram, since it was his ashram I would be visiting in Rishikesh. For about an hour, while boxes were being packed into the trunk of the car, I watched the life around me in this ashram. Someone handed me a bottle of water. I had no idea how one says "Thank you" in India, so I placed both my hands in prayer position and said, "Namaste." I hoped I wouldn't go wrong with this greeting that means "I salute the divine in you."

It was five o'clock when we left the ashram in Delhi to continue our journey to Rishikesh. The drive was long and the road bumpy. I thanked God I was wearing my sports bra because the ride was so shaky I would have had to hold my breasts for the next six hours!

Everything we passed looked so unfamiliar I felt as though I were watching a movie. The clothes, the houses, the roads, the people—everything was new to me. Wonderfully colorful saris made the women appear elegant and beautiful. The children looked happier than any I have ever seen, despite their great poverty. There were elephants and monkeys and, always, the constantly blowing horns.

On the radio someone was singing the "Song of a Toothache," at least that's what it sounded like to my Western ears. I wanted to ask my driver to turn down the volume but was afraid he wouldn't understand me and, besides, the music seemed to help him concentrate. Concentration is critical when you drive in India. For me, who is accustomed to Western traffic rules, it seemed as though every driver wanted to commit suicide. Whenever our driver changed his course at the last minute, I had no idea which system or criteria he was following. It made me think of the bumper cars at a fair, which have to move quickly before they crash as the drivers test one another to see who has the strongest nerves.

I took a sip out of my water bottle and reminded myself to drink carefully. Who knows where one goes to the bathroom in India, I thought, and how do I tell the driver? My questions were answered an hour later by the side of the road, where—thank God—there were enough bushes.

After we had been on the road for three hours, we stopped again by the side of the road, this time at a kind of street cafe. The ubiquitous Coca-cola sign hung above a tent that gave some shade in the growing heat. Underneath there was a counter with a square bench in front, and a huge, round metal bowl in which some food was being fried. My travel companions were hungry and, when I thought about it, so was I. They signaled with a hand sign that I should have some breakfast with them. A little stiff from sitting so long, I climbed out of the car and found myself a place on the bench.

My driver asked me something I didn't understand. I decided to nod "Yes" anyway. This was exciting. What, I wondered, had I agreed to?

It turned out to be a metal plate and a bottle of Coca-cola. The fork was lying over something square and beige. What could that be? I knew every traveler is instructed never, ever to taste anything in a foreign country that has been prepared in a questionable manner. But that had never bothered me. I ate salad in Egypt, chicken from a market in Marrakech and sweet desserts in Mombasa without ever having any problems. I like to try new things, so I took a bite of this beige square. Wow, it tasted good! I had no idea what it was, but I ate two of them.

While I was waiting for my driver, I looked around. I felt great joy to be on this journey, joy to be in India—a land where women and men of God are honored. It was such a different feeling from being in the United States or Germany. I enjoyed the trust I felt, and the comfort to travel without any worries.

Back in the car, we resumed our shaky journey—as well as the toothache music. I still had my earplugs from the plane, so I put them in and the sound of the music became an acceptable hum.

Finally we reached Rishikesh. Once again my luggage disappeared, except for the bag with my altar and sacred pipe, which I never let go from my sight. As my body slowly readjusted to standing upright, I was guided into the ashram. Everything was clean and peaceful. In the center of the ashram different scenes had been constructed from the Bhagavad Gita, the holy book of India that can be compared with the Bible. As I observed the colorful jewels and vivid painting on the different statues, I was reminded that the Hindu religion is very bright and joyful. Since I was accustomed to the solemn reverence of the Catholic Church, it was a bit like being in a festive market place.

I didn't have much time to look around, however, because Swami Chidanand Saraswati, also called Swami Muniji, was

waiting for me. The honor of being personally greeted by him had nothing to do with me, but was due to Jacqueline Snyder, who had been friends with him for many years.

First I was asked to take off my shoes. Then a young man directed me to an inner sanctuary where Swami Muniji was sitting on a cream-colored mattress on the floor. In front of him was a low table with some paper and pencils. Behind him were three phones. Men in business suits sat before him, listening carefully to what he said and nodding frequently.

Swami Muniji smiled at me and gestured for me to sit down. He wore orange and his long, dark hair was down to his shoulders. He was small and delicate and had open, happy eyes that reminded me of the eyes of a child. He enjoys his life, I thought, one can see it in his face.

As I watched the swami and his guests, I tried to imagine what they were talking about. Some of his guests sat cross-legged, while others were on their knees and yet others on their heels, toes stretched to the floor. After about ten minutes, everyone stood up, put their hands in front of them, palms together, bowed a couple of times and left the room.

Swami Muniji gave me a warm smile. "Welcome home."

"I am very happy to be here."

"Your friends were missing you. I hope you were not worried on your way to Rishikesh."

"I am with God; how could I be worried?"

He seemed to like my answer. "Good, good," he said. "We meet everyone for lunch at one o'clock. You are my guest."

I stood, folded my hands and bowed.

Outside, Swami Muniji's personal secretary was waiting to bring me to my room. I followed him up the stairs to the first floor, where I stopped to view the Ganges, the holy river of India that flows in front of the ashram. I stayed there for a moment and took in the magnificence of the scene.

With friendly patience, the swami's secretary waited until I signaled that I was ready to continue. We went up to the second floor, where he opened one of the doors. I could feel the vibration of my friends as soon as I walked in. There were three adjoining rooms, with four beds made up with clean blankets and inviting pillows. Everything was very simple. I could tell by the travel altars which of the beds belonged to my friends: Sheila's angel statue was on a green shawl; Sharon had her three ceremonial pipes on a lavender cloth; Linda had a violet cloth and a couple of fairy pictures. The empty room I assumed was for me.

This was my first ashram visit and I was curious what would happen to me. Every time I go on a spiritual journey, I want to learn something. I want to break through old limitations. So I prayed, "Dear God, I am here in India to learn, to grow, to see more and understand more and to remember who I am and what I can be. I want to know more about You and Your angels. I am ready, please teach me!"

I took a deep breath and sent out my prayer, my deepest wish and highest concentration. I knew that all my wishes are fulfilled if I send with them the necessary power and intent. My power is my sincere desire to find truth. I have learned that reality is created out of two elements: the first is our wishes; the second, our actions. For this reason, I spend time with wishes and day dreaming. When I have made the effort to imagine how I would like my life to be, my actions and reactions can more readily create my reality in accordance with my wishes.

It was almost time for lunch, so I went in search of a shower, which I found nearby. After I had washed myself, I felt ready for the next adventure. But I also noticed my mood was not as happy as it had been earlier. Shouldn't I be extremely ecstatic after a shower, especially considering I had been on the road for almost two days? But I was feeling somewhat melancholy, and I wondered why.

Just then my friends came into the room and my mood swing was interrupted by hugs and kisses. Linda, Sharon, Sheila and Jacqueline, Nancy and Perry, a couple from San Diego, all greeted me. Since we have all traveled together, both on inside journeys and outside journeys, I was very happy to see them. Unlike me, they had just spent the past week in silence and were ready to reenter the outer world. In my case, I had arrived a week late and whatever spiritual enlightenment was to come my way would have only eight days to do its work.

After lunch I became more acutely aware of how mercurial my mood was. Swami Muniji wanted to show us his hospital. I understood what a great honor this was. Because of Swami Muniji's status in India, this gesture could be considered equivalent to the Pope showing us his private chapel. Nevertheless, I found myself holding myself at a distance. On the way to the hospital, we passed a little garden he wanted to show us. Reluctantly I followed the group. "Get yourself together," I demanded of myself. "What's the matter with you?"

But that didn't help. I couldn't just "get myself together." I preferred to disappear and be by myself. That desire became stronger and stronger, so I leaned against a tree and closed my eyes to meditate. I imagined that I was leaving my body. But this time I couldn't do it. The only thing that happened was that I felt a restlessness that grew from a soft breeze into a full-blown storm. I also had the desire to scratch myself all over.

I finally admitted to myself that I had to be alone. I walked over to Swami Muniji. After all, who else if not the Guru of an ashram would understand that I needed silence and time alone? I tried to be as respectful as possible as I apologized for myself. "I'm very sorry," I said, "but I must excuse myself. I am in need of silence."

Swami Muniji looked at me with surprise, but he seemed to understand. He nodded, folded his hands and bowed. I also folded my hands and bowed. Then, without looking at my friends, I walked with swift steps back to the ashram.

Some minutes later I lay completely clothed in my bed, the covers pulled over my head, and I cried. I had not the slightest idea why, but that didn't stop my tears. I don't know how long I lay there, but finally I heard my friends returning. I turned my head to the wall and could hear them whisper to each other so they wouldn't disturb me. Each of them understood the need for time alone with oneself. They could see that this was my time to be alone and to speak with God—because it was from Him that my answers would come.

So I turned to God. "Turn" is probably not the right expression; I screamed at God: "Why don't I hear God all the time?" I knew it was possible to hear God and your angels all the time. Jacqueline, for example, did it constantly. I, on the other hand, had to first close my eyes, meditate and then search for the inner answers. I wanted every thought I had to be sent from God, to be connected with God. I wanted to experience constant contact with God. But how? Again, I closed my eyes and asked my angels to show themselves.

But nothing happened. Again and again, I cried: "Where are you?"

In my inner eye, there was only darkness. I felt only self-pity. Wasn't I doing enough?

I stood up and left my room. I walked by some monks who were praying, past some holy cows, past the Ganges. I followed a little pathway into the nearby forest. The tears were running down my cheeks but I did nothing to stop them. I didn't care how I looked or what the others thought of me. My only wish was to have God always close to me. I screamed aloud, demanding: "God, where are You?"

I started to get angry at myself. If God wasn't listening to me, I must be doing something wrong. But what? Was my love not big enough? I wanted to know. I lay down flat on the earth and tried to make a deal with God: "What do You want from me? Do You want me to change my life?"

No answer.

"Do You want me to spend more time alone?"

No answer.

"Do You want me to change my profession?"

No answer.

For hours and hours I called on God. I searched for my angels. But nobody answered. Even the wind, who always communicated with me, was quiet.

"Brother wind, help me please," I begged in a whisper. I was sitting with my feet in the Ganges and my eyes closed. There was no movement from the wind, no answer, nothing. The more I searched, the more I asked for God, the quieter it became.

Finally I went back to my room. I felt a deep sadness, as though I had failed at something. A part of me could not believe I hadn't received any information. I knew my an-

gels were always with me, but why couldn't I feel them? I knew God was everywhere, but why couldn't I hear Him? I was so immersed in my questions, I didn't notice Jacqueline standing calmly next to my bed. She looked like a princess from the fairy-tale "1001 Nights." Her thick, black hair flowed in long curls, untamed, around her ageless face. Her pink sari matched her lipstick. As I looked at her I thought how she loved eye makeup and colorful jewelry. She loved life, with all its glory, colors and joy.

She looked gently down at me. "How are you?" she asked tenderly.

Tears poured down my face and I sobbed, "Not good."

She sat down on the corner of my bed and hugged me. As I felt her arms around my shoulder, I sobbed even more. She rocked me like a baby in her arms. Slowly I stopped crying. I looked for a handkerchief.

"Here." Jacqueline passed me hers.

I dried my face and blew my nose.

"Would you like to talk about it?" she asked.

I nodded and looked into Jacqueline's dark, wise eyes. Yes, I thought, she can hear her angels. Sometimes when she spoke, she stopped in the middle of a sentence and listened, and then she laughed, as if she had just heard something incredible funny. Her inner dialogs were filled with wisdom, explanations, visions and never-ending questions. Each time I watched her, I wanted to experience what she experienced. There was no jealousy; I wanted her to have what she had. I just wanted to have it, too. "I want to hear God the way you do," I said, and with these words I started to cry again.

Jacqueline smiled. I could feel her love deep inside of me and I knew she understood my spirit.

"I'm ready to do anything for that," I said, "but I can't hear anything. Where is God? Why are my angels quiet? Even the wind won't speak to me anymore. What have I done wrong? I've flown all the way to India and I hear less here than I did in L.A. What am I not getting? Why is God not with me?" I wrung my handkerchief with my hands.

Jacqueline hugged me again. She rocked me slowly in her arms. Then she said a wonderful, fantastic, unbelievable, explanatory sentence: "The more you ask God 'Where are You?' the further you send Him away."

Of course! How dumb of me! I knew my thoughts created my reality. So if I believed I were alone, then I would be alone. If I believed God were far away, He would be far away! In the truest sense of the word, a light bulb went off in my head and I finally got it.

I thanked Jacqueline and jumped up. I took my journal and ran back to the forest. I stretched out my arms and with deep humility I said, "God, here I am." And in my head I heard loud and clear: "And here am I."

Yes! That was what I had needed to learn. If I were looking for God that meant I had somehow *lost* Him. But one can't lose God, one can only lose oneself.

"Should I change my life? Should I give up something?" I wanted to know.

"Why?" I heard in my mind. "Would you love God more? Would you love the people you live with more? Would you be more of service without the things that are part of your life?"

"No." That was true, I wouldn't. It might be easier to find God, to be of service, in an ashram, but shouldn't we also be of service to God and the people in the midst of our daily life? Isn't it true that our spirituality stretches from the twenty minutes of meditation to the entire twenty-four hours of a day? That way, we not only know about spirituality, but we truly are living it.

"Is there anything you would like from me?" I asked in my thoughts.

"Discipline."

Discipline? "Is there a discipline that would help my learning?"

"Yes."

"I'm ready."

"Wake up, pray and meditate between three and four in the morning for an hour. Write afterward. Wake your child at seven and have breakfast with your family. Work until noon. Eat raw vegetables and bread for lunch. Take a nap outside and sleep on the earth until you wake up. Dance and move your energy. Pick up your daughter from school and spend time with her. Cook with love for your husband. When the sun sets, go outside and pray. Go to bed when you are tired."

I opened my eyes and wrote everything down in my journal. I remembered waking up early as I was writing my first book. That was my best time to be creative. I also love to sleep outside on the earth. Dancing I consider a waste of time because I always think I could be doing something more important. And, what a surprise that I have to cook again, a task that a few years ago I had passed on to our housekeeper Esther. At lunch Swami Muniji had told us he only eats what has been cooked for him with love. "Everything is energy," he had said.

I was a little concerned about my sleep time. I remembered that last year I was always counting the hours: Let's see, I slept four hours during the night, so I need to have at

least two hours during my nap otherwise I will be tired during the day. I asked: "How much sleep do I need?"

"Where is your focus?"

I thought for a second. "How much sleep I should get."

"Would you like to keep your focus there?"

"No," I answered. "My focus is service, not sleep."

"Sleep will find you," I heard inside. "You don't have to
search for it."

As always, I wondered, "But I have appointments. I have
to make plans. How do I know when my body is tired? What
if I have a very important appointment?" Without waiting
for an answer, I knew deep inside that I will never miss an
important date or appointment because I am tired. Why?
Because that would not serve my intention.

The sun went down and I lay flat on the earth to pray. I
picked up a stone that lay next to me and held it in my hand.
I would take it home with me to remind me of this wonderful day. I placed a piece of my hair where the stone had
been. I never take anything from nature without leaving
something in return.

I closed my eyes and thanked God for this day. What a
wonderful lesson I had received. It would bring me to my
goal to become the best person I could be.

Discipline: who would have thought it was so important? But isn't it clear? Discipline is concentration.
Wherever we concentrate, wherever our focus is, that
becomes energy. Whatever we do with the energy will
be realized. If I use my energy to gossip, then gossip is
a large part of my life. If I use my energy for sports,
then sports become a large part of my life. If I use my
energy to complain, then complaining is a large part of
my life. If I use a large part of the focus on my job, then

the job is a large part of my life. If I focus on God, then God is a large part of my life.

It was dark when I returned to the Ganges. I wanted to close the day with a ritual, so my angels sent me to the holy river. I didn't know why I was being sent to the river, but I trusted my intuition and that they would show me the right rituals.

"Stand in the river," I heard. I took off my shoes and wrapped my sari even closer around my hips. I waded knee-deep into the cool Ganges. I held the stone I had found earlier in the water and a vow formulated in my head: "For love and commitment."

I took the stone out of the water and held it to my heart. I took a deep breath in. I felt I should place it down into the water again. "For discipline," I heard myself whisper.

Again I took the stone from the river onto my heart. For the third time I bowed down and wet the stone. "Thy will over my will."

I felt the stone on my heart. It was strong, determined, as old as the world itself. Then it came into my mind that I should ask God for His oath to me. I dipped the stone into the water and held it up to the starry sky: "For your love and your commitment."

As I held my arms straight upward, I felt the wind getting stronger. Tears ran down my cheeks. I was full of joy and humility. Thank God! Thank God! A second time I dipped the stone into the water and held it up with outstretched arms. I said, "For discipline." And I waited for the wind. But it was quiet. I had to smile. Discipline, I figured, is not a problem for God.

I took the stone for the third time and dipped it in the water. This time I lifted my arm and stretched it far out:

"Thy will over my will." Once again, I felt the wind, my brother.

I don't know how long I stood in the Ganges and watched the movement of this holy river. This river is Mother India. Here one cleans the body, one prays, one brings flowers and one sends the dead on their final journey. But the holy river also has much dirt in it because no one wants to clean it up. If you clean up dirt in India, you become an untouchable, the lowest rung in the caste system. This traditional hierarchy of the Hindu religion is one of the biggest problems in India. Swami Muniji started to clean the streets himself once a week because if one who is a living God can clean them without becoming an untouchable, others can do so as well. What a wonderful example he offered to help his land.

I thanked my angels and God for the love and wisdom that came into me.

"Be like the river," I heard in me. "Nothing can bother it. Nothing changes its course. Take the negativity, take the dirt, as the Ganges does, and bring it back and leave it on the shore. Just follow your way. Be like the river: strong, quiet and determined."

The next day I woke up shortly before four o'clock and went to the temple for my morning meditation. Having never been to a Hindu temple before, I looked around with curiosity. Since it was too early for the Hindu morning prayer, there was no one else around. I left my shoes in front of the door and quietly walked across the stone floor to the center of the temple. Many small mats had been placed on the floor so one could sit in prayer. In front was a kind of stage and in the middle a glass shrine containing a wax statue of the re-

cently passed Shri Swami Shukadevanandaji Maharaj, who had founded the ashram and then eight years ago given it to his pupil Swami Muniji.

This was the first day of my new discipline, a very important day for me. It was the beginning of my commitment to God, my promise to Him. I felt as though I had just climbed a mountain and now I was enjoying the view. I had no idea a new mountain would appear soon.

I spent the morning without talking. Swami Muniji expected us at noon for lunch. We were served freshly prepared dishes, each like a Christmas present. Then he suggested we visit the holy city of Hardware, only a short distance from the ashram. Within five minutes Jacqueline and he had decided who would drive which car and who would ride with whom. "Okay then," I heard Jacqueline say. "Let's meet at two o'clock in front of the office."

Normally this would be the time for my nap, so I said, "I think I'd rather stay here."

Jacqueline looked surprised: "Sabrina, this is a wonderful city. You wouldn't want to miss it. It is one of the holiest cities of India. The temples are absolutely fantastic."

Immediately I thought, Jacqueline probably knows more than I do. Maybe the angels have told her I should come with her. I'll just lie down for half an hour and then I won't mind driving with them. "Okay," I said, "I'll come with you."

Almost immediately I felt uncomfortable with this decision. But I chose to ignore the feeling and go along with Jacqueline's suggestion. I went to my room and lay down on my bed. But I couldn't fall asleep. Soon my friends came in and it was time to get ready for the trip.

The drive to Hardware, which was supposed to take only forty-five minutes, took much longer. It was hotter than usual, and the temples didn't mean much to me. Because we were the only tourists many beggars crowded around us in the busy marketplace.

Later I heard about Hardware's famous Kumbha Mela, the festival for which the holy masters come down from the mountains once every twelve years so they can meet and share their wisdom. The vibration of love and mastery is said to be incredible and still palpable throughout the following years. But I was very tired and couldn't feel anything close to such a vibration. I went back to the car and tried to sleep. The only thought that came to me through this unhappiness was: Why hadn't I stayed at the ashram?

Back in my room, tired, angry and dusty, I sat in front of my altar and prayed, "Dear God, my angels, what didn't I get this time?"

The answer from my angels was so clear and logical I was surprised I hadn't thought of it earlier: "You have to listen to your own intuition. Always ask God first. Don't make any decisions according to what other people do or say, even if you trust them with your life. They base their decisions on their intuition and you have to base your decisions on yours."

It was true. I admired Jacqueline's integrity, her love of God, her service to people, her respect for nature and her commitment. But my admiration for others had to be balanced with admiration for myself. I also have God's spark in me. My daily life, my positive thoughts, my words and my actions make this light brighter and brighter. There will always be people who are an inspiration to me, but I cannot follow them. I can only follow God.

I opened my eyes. From my window I could see the sun

going down. Yes, I thought, the goal for everyone is the same, but our roads are different.

This lesson had been my second mountain.

58

Chapter Four

**About an Angel who appeared as a human and
how important our first thoughts are in the morning**

As the plane flew over Asia, on my way home, I thanked my angels for their help. I always enjoy flying alone because I have this time all to myself. I even look forward to the unexpected incidents that happen on my trips because they are what makes life interesting.

The young man sitting next to me playing a computer game reminded me of Brandon, one of Jaqueline's sons. Last year, Brandon had flown alone for the first time. He was fifteen years old and he wanted to visit his father, who is a musician and who was touring in the Philippines.

As I put my airplane seat in a more comfortable position, I remembered a conversation we'd had when Brandon and his mother came over to talk about my first trip to Asia. "My angel materialized as I flew to Manila," he told me between cleaning up the table and putting the dishes into the dishwasher.

"What?" I stood midway between the refrigerator and the sink and stared at him.

Brandon looked like a real teenager in his blue T-shirt and blue pants. He stared directly back at me and said, "He materialized himself. I mean, he sat next to me in the airplane."

"Aha." I don't know what surprised me more: that he saw an angel materialize itself, or that he was a teenager

who talked about such experiences.

Brandon grinned at me the way only a real teenager grins. "You've obviously never had an experience like that," he observed.

That was true.

"Well," he said, hoisting himself onto the kitchen counter, "I wanted to visit my father in Manila and my Mom couldn't go with me. So we decided I would go by myself. You know, when you fly from the West Coast it is a really long journey and I was a little nervous because I had to change planes in Taiwan. When I boarded the plane in Seattle, I felt a knot in my stomach. In the seat next to me was an Asian man wearing a blue-green sports jacket with his name engraved over the heart. His name was Gil. He smiled at me very kindly and I suddenly had a funny feeling inside. Something in me was happy this man was sitting there. We started to talk. You know, in the tourist section one always sits very close, so I could feel him."

"What do you mean 'feel' him?" I asked.

"You know how it feels when someone sits next to you and you just feel comfortable around that person. You know what I mean—this soft feeling inside. I felt completely secure and very well taken care of with him. So we flew to Taiwan and during the trip he told me all about Manila, because he was going there, too. He had been born there and he was visiting his family. He told me about the different customs of the country, where I should go shopping and what I should bring home and what to do when you meet someone, and all sorts of things." Brandon jumped down from the kitchen counter and continued, "So I landed in Taiwan and, thanks to his help, I had no problems changing planes. The amazing thing was, when I walked onto the next plane, I discovered I had been upgraded. My seat was in first class."

I was surprised. "Did you talk to anyone to get upgraded to first class?"

Brandon shook his head. "Nope. I didn't do anything. Actually I had never flown first class so I didn't know you could do that. Besides—can you imagine—my neighbor who had been sitting next to me in coach was also sitting with me in first class. And right next to me again!"

"That's fantastic."

Brandon grinned in agreement. "It was fantastic. So I landed in Manila, my dad picked me up and I never really thought about that guy again. Not until I flew back home. I was alone again, but this time I wasn't worried because it was my second time. And guess who was on the plane with me?"

"The man from Manila."

"Exactly. But this time he sat a couple of rows behind me. It was as though I didn't need so much help anymore because now I knew my way. But he was still somewhere there in case I should need him. Isn't that cool, or what?"

"Yes, 'cool' is the right expression for that." I watched Brandon as he popped a tomato in his mouth and thought to myself how naturally he spoke about these experiences. For him there was no question but that it had been his guardian angel who traveled with him and took care of him. But was it truly his guardian angel? I notice that I had this thought: Well, do I believe this is possible?

Then I heard my angel in my head: "Your belief creates your reality. Brandon believed this is possible and that is why it happened for him. Do you believe this is possible?"

I looked around the plane. The young man next to me

was still playing his computer game. The couple to my left were obviously in the middle of a heated argument. I glanced over all the seats. Some people were asleep, others were talking and yet others were wearing headphones to watch the movie. Just then an elderly lady half way down the aisle turned her head toward me, gave me a wise smile and winked. I had a funny feeling inside. Was she? Maybe?

The next morning I woke up in my own bed. It is my habit every morning to stay in bed for awhile and count my blessings. My first thoughts in the morning used to be about something unhappy or uncomfortable, or something I hadn't finished. I thought of all the people I had to call, the things I had to do, or a talk I hadn't prepared. These things would create a knot in my stomach. And, of course, that took care of my mood for the whole day.

Now when I wake up I count my blessings: I thank my body; I thank my health, my husband and my daughter, my sisters and my friends, my animals, my home and my freedom. I thank God, my angels and my spiritual teachers for their presence in my life. I thank Jesus and Zarathustra, my spirit guide Gray Wolf, an old Indian wise man and my white eagle. Then I wish for my daughter Julia to have all the teachers and all the angels she needs to guide her through life. Finally I thank God for this new day and for all the challenges I will face, and I reaffirm my commitment to learn and become a better person—the best person I can be in God's service. With that, my whole day begins in a more determined, more joyful and more humble way than it did before.

By counting my blessings, I'm reminded of how wonderful my life is. There is always something in life for which we can be thankful; there is always something that is a blessing. Even in the worst moments we can find something wonderful. It may only be something very small, but the more we concentrate on it, the better we feel. In this way, we can shift ourselves into a different mood.

It was dark when I woke up. Glancing at the clock by my bedside, I noticed it was almost four o'clock. It was easy to stay with my new discipline now that I was at home. I brushed my teeth, washed my face and put on some comfortable clothes. It was quiet in the house with everyone asleep. No phones were ringing and no one was around to disturb me.

In our old house, I had a little blue room where I meditated. This room, however, was not always blue. It used to be the maid's room, with a small closet and a tiny table in the corner next to the bed. Five years ago, when I started to meditate, I had the desire to create my own meditation space. So I made this extra room my meditation room. I painted the walls blue, and it became my blue room.

In that house, my office was separate from my meditation room. But when we moved to our new house, I knew I would have to work where I prayed. The guest house in the new house used to be a professional music study, with thick walls and a sunken floor. It had two adjoining rooms: one for the technical equipment and the technicians, and the other for the musicians. When we bought the house, I knew immediately this would be my studio. The walls were filled with the memory of beautiful music—how appropriate for a room of prayer, reverence and meditation. Besides, I urgently needed more room because I no longer had enough space for the meditation groups and workshops I gave.

I took everything out of the recording studio until there were just the bare walls. Then I started to build different level, until I had created a wonderful feeling in this huge room. The walls were painted a soft cream color and the largest wall I painted blue with large waves, like the water—representing life, movement, change, silence. I cut the legs off a little desk so I could put it on the floor and sit cross-legged to work on my computer. I placed this desk in front of the large sliding glass doors so I could look outside and see the hills on the other side of the canyon.

That morning, I opened the glass door and put on my house slippers as I entered the studio. I turned on the little light next to my desk and sat cross-legged before my altar. On the altar were pictures of Jesus, Zarathustra, Shiva and St. Francis of Assisi; a statue of Buddha; paintings of angels and numerous crystals. My sacred pipe, wrapped in red cloth, a bowl of water, a candle and an abalone shell with sweet grass and sage were also laid out on the altar, along with some feathers, stones and earth from places I had visited and where I had prayed.

I lit my candle and I burned some sage. I moved the smoke gently around my body with a feather and thought about letting go of old negative habits. I have learned from Native Americans to use the smoke of sage to cleanse myself, much as I would wash my hands before eating.

I closed my eyes and spoke my prayer: "Dear God, dear angels, beloved spirits, thank you for my trip to India and for all my experiences. I am embracing the new discipline with joy and am ready today to learn something new."

Then I imagined God's light shining down on me. It was bright, warm and full of love and I imagined it going deeper and deeper through the top of my head into my body. It moved slowly down my spine and stopped at the base. I saw the light come forward like a spiral, going up from the base of my spine to my heart, passing my throat and my third eye and coming back into my head. I imagined all that because I know my imagination guides this light exactly where I want it. I let the light stay in my brain and circle around. After awhile I let it pass out through the top of my head and move upward. I felt as though I had just taken an inner shower. I let myself be quiet, enjoying the peace inside. Sometimes in my meditations I feel just a beingness, a feeling of being fully alive and being quiet at the same time. There are no thoughts, just the feeling of comfort, as it was that morning.

66

Chapter Five

About Angels who care for animals and what happens if God becomes your father

After a while, I could hear Samantha in my thoughts. She had a wonderful voice. She spoke with so much love and caring you automatically wanted to cuddle up in her arms and be taken care of by her. No wonder all the animals wanted to come close to her.

I got to know Samantha when I attended a conference of visionaries in Washington, organized by Jacqueline Snyder, the founder of Sacred Life. The list of speakers was long and impressive. Dr. Valerie Hunt, a former professor at the University of California in Los Angeles, spoke about energy fields. David Berry, a member of the United States Bureau, spoke about the environment. Robert Dean, a former NATO officer, spoke about UFOs. Don Alejandro, a shaman from the Amazon jungle who had never been out of Peru spoke, and so did Harry Charger, a Native American wisdom keeper. Samantha Khury talked about how to communicate with animals.

I loved this conference. Along with one hundred equally curious, like-minded people, I had a wonderful time over this long weekend. Samantha stood out even among all these exceptional people. I felt as though we had known each other for many lifetimes. She looked like an angel: gentle, blond curls, light blue eyes. Her movements were harmonious and her expression was open, friendly and understanding. Al-

though she was around fifty years old, she looked very young. She had an aura of confidence that people get when they know about themselves.

The conference center was about two hours from the airport. It so happened that Samantha and I drove back together after the conference in my rental car. We were barely on the freeway when I asked her to tell me more about herself.

"I was born out of wedlock. My mother was a teenager," she shared. "Back then, that was terrible for the whole family. My mother was too young to take care of me, so first my grandfather raised me. When I was five years old, my aunt, my mother's second oldest sister, took me from the house I had known as my home and brought me into her family. It was a very traumatic transition." She paused, then added, "No one ever, ever talked about my father. There was an unwritten law about that in my family. Even as a little child I never asked any questions about my father."

"Have you had a lot of thoughts about him?"

"Yes, he was always in my fantasies. I would imagine how he looked, and what he would tell me. Then one day after church—I must have been about five years old—the priest asked me as I left the church: 'Do you not know who your father is?'"

"Did he talk to you about your father?" I asked her, trying to keep my eyes on the traffic.

"Wait," Samantha said with a smile. "I said, 'No' and my heart started to pound. I thought to myself, finally someone is going to tell me about my father." Samantha looked out the window for a minute, then continued, "The priest said, 'God is your father.' I said to myself, 'God is my father! No wonder no one in my family talks about him.'"

I laughed. "Well, you must have thought you and Jesus were in the same boat."

"Exactly," replied Samantha. "God is my father. And whenever I pray, I speak to my father, because that is what a priest told me."

"Did you ever tell your family that you found out who your father was?"

"No, no. I was very happy knowing God was my father," Samantha asserted. "From then on my life was easier. God was my father. Even if I was sad or lonely—which very often I was—deep inside me was the knowledge that God, my father, was always there for me."

What a marvelous thought, I said to myself. This child, who often felt lonely and missed her parents, sudden learned from a priest that God was her father. I could imagine what influence this must have had on her life.

"Since I can remember, I was always surrounded by animals who needed help," she continued. "Even as a very young girl, sick animals would appear. Birds flew from the trees when I walked by, hurt porcupines stopped in my path and little field mice were too weak to run away."

She smiled and explained further: "I was raised Christian and I know how often the Bible is interpreted in different ways. But I was told that if you try to heal someone, you give the devil an opportunity to work through you. What could I do? When I found a hurt bird whose wings needed healing, my heart told me to me to pick it up and lay my hands around its shaky little body. But my mind said, 'Don't do it, you might do something terrible.'" She shook her shoulders. "I had so much desire to help that I asked God, my father, for His assistance. Then I would immediately feel my hands getting warmer and my love streaming through my hands, like a warm blanket that enveloped the bird. Whenever I focused on my heart and my wish to help, my hands would become very hot."

"How old were you then?" I asked.

She thought about it. "I must have been about five or six years old. Maybe younger. But I remember that every time I helped an animal, I felt two huge figures behind me. One on my right side and one on my left."

"Huge figures?"

"Yes. I didn't realize at the time that they were angels. These figures were very close to me. I felt as if I'd always known them. Every time I felt them, I would look behind and above me because I expected to see someone standing there. But no one was ever there—I mean, no one I could see."

"Did you feel some sort of wind movement, or a touch?"

"No." Samantha shook her head. "It was more as if someone I knew had come from behind and was looking over my shoulder. I remember how surprised I was every time I looked up and couldn't see anyone there. I felt my angels so strongly I expected them to be there so I could see them! " She laughed softly. "Now I understand that they were there to encourage me to continue, to let me know that what I was doing was rightful and good. Whenever they appeared, my hands would get warmer and warmer. A short time later, the hurt bird would shake his wings and fly away."

I was fascinated. "All sorts of people must have brought you their animals."

"Oh, no," Samantha replied. "I never talked about this with anyone. Remember, I wasn't sure I was supposed to be

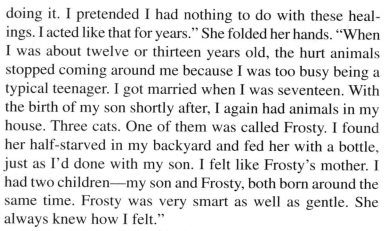

doing it. I pretended I had nothing to do with these healings. I acted like that for years." She folded her hands. "When I was about twelve or thirteen years old, the hurt animals stopped coming around me because I was too busy being a typical teenager. I got married when I was seventeen. With the birth of my son shortly after, I again had animals in my house. Three cats. One of them was called Frosty. I found her half-starved in my backyard and fed her with a bottle, just as I'd done with my son. I felt like Frosty's mother. I had two children—my son and Frosty, both born around the same time. Frosty was very smart as well as gentle. She always knew how I felt."

Samantha's smile suddenly turned to sadness. "When I was about twenty-five, my life took another sharp turn. One day I took Frosty to the vet. She hadn't eaten for a couple of days, and I noticed that the skin around her mouth had moved backward and I could look deep down in her throat. Every morning this empty spot got larger until she had difficulty even drinking. I had Frosty on my lap, and the vet looked at her very closely. He told me there was no hope for Frosty. She had a disease that meant the cells around her mouth were dying, leaving a deep hole that would get larger and larger. The end result would be death by starvation. The vet told me to avoid further pain I should have her put to sleep that same day."

Samantha's voice started to shake. I took my eyes quickly off the traffic and glanced over at her. She had tears in her eyes but she wasn't resisting them. When she had spoken at the conference, I had also noticed she didn't distance herself from her feelings. She just had them. I, on the other hand, always tried to rise above my feelings so other people won't know how I felt and so I could avoid embarrassment

in case I started crying. I thought that if one cried, one was weak. But there was nothing weak about Samantha's tears. This was the natural expression of her love for Frosty.

I was torn. What should I do now? Should I give her a handkerchief? Should I say something? But what? Should I pretend I didn't see her tears? Should I change the subject?

Samantha just let her tears roll down her cheeks. I noticed a burning sensation in my own eyes, as if I felt her pain in my heart. First I wanted to stop these feelings. "Are you going crazy?" I heard in my head. My eyes filled with tears and my thoughts were with Frosty's and Samantha's pain. I decided to let those feelings come in. This was strange for me. For the first time, I didn't feel weak because I was crying. I felt a certain strength. I felt awake and somehow larger, somehow stronger. There was a sense of harmony in my crying, as if it was supposed to be that way.

Samantha's voice came back into my ear: "I stared at my vet in sheer horror. My Frosty? Put her to sleep? She was like my second child; I couldn't possibly do that. I held Frosty even closer to my chest. I cried and cried and ran out of the office. The vet shook his head at my emotional reaction and yelled after me: 'What you're doing is cruel. Your animal will suffer unnecessarily.'"

"My whole body shook as I drove home. Frosty looked at me with her smart eyes. Then, from deep inside myself, the memories of my childhood emerged. I remembered how my hands would get hot when I held a sick animal. Nothing was more important than to get that feeling back, and to know and trust that Frosty could get completely healthy again."

I wiped my tears off my face with the back of my hand. Samantha's tears continued to flow gracefully down her chin onto her folded hands. She said, "When I got home, I sat Frosty on my lap, her head on my knees and her behind touching my belly. I gently laid my hands around her head. I prayed and prayed with all the power and concentration, all the love and focus I had and all the desire I felt: 'I ask you my beloved Father, God. Please send me Your heavenly power so Frosty can be healed. If You heal my beloved Frosty, I promise I will find out why I have this gift with my hands. I will use my talent to help You and serve You in the world. I will do whatever I have to do until I die, I swear. In the name of Lord, Jesus Christ. Amen.' From the deepest place in my heart, I asked God to allow the warmth to come through my hands again."

She stopped crying. "Then I felt it again. My two large angels. I felt their bodies gently touching mine like a tender hug. I felt confident everything would be all right. 'Continue, continue. Trust your instinct'; these were the thoughts that came into my head, loud and clear. And then my hands started to get warmer."

She smiled at me. "Three times a day I laid my hands on Frosty. Every morning right after I woke up, I put Frosty on my lap, laid my hands around her head and spoke my prayer. I felt my hands get warmer and Frosty would start to purr. At lunch time and in the evening, I did the same thing with her. Each time it was for a half hour, and each time she gave me this wonderful purring I loved so much. I did this for three days. On the third day—it was during my lunch break—I felt my hands become wet from her saliva. She purred more deeply than I'd ever heard before. Then Frosty turned around and looked at me directly. She pushed her head deep into my stomach, as if she were trying to say thanks. I started to cry. There was a mixture of joy and humility. I knew something powerful had happened and that Frosty would be completely healed. Not only had something important happened in Frosty's life, but also in mine."

Again, Samantha's eyes filled with tears. I was fascinated by the normal way in which she dealt with her feelings. "I watched Frosty," she continued. "She jumped down from my lap and went to her food bowl. She started to eat! After seven days, she started to eat again!"

She looked happily in my direction. "You know, Sabrina, because of Frosty, I finally started to consider my talent as a healer. I knew it was a gift from God and wanted to find someone who could help me learn more about it. I explored what was available and ended up in a school that taught about color and energy. It was called *actualism*. I learned that the body was more than just a combination of tissues, organs and blood. I studied at that school for about seventeen years and learned how to do massage and how to use energy for healing. My clients were humans who were looking for other ways to become healthy."

"But how did you start to talk with animals?"

"That was about fifteen years after Frosty had been healed. I must have been in my late thirties. One day my oldest son brought home a pheasant that had been hit by a car. He was unhurt but in shock. I had the impression the pheasant truly believed he was going to die. I took some chairs from the patio and made him a kind of cage. I didn't want to confine him, just give him the feeling he had his own space. I laid my hand around the pheasant's body, but there was no reaction. The next morning, after my children had left the house, I sat down with the pheasant and closed my eyes. I spoke

my prayer: "Dear God, my Father, please allow me to be one with this animal so I can tell him that he is unharmed, that he can fly away, that he has nothing broken, that he can trust his ability to fly and that he can get back his joy of flying."

Samantha closed her eyes as she sat next to me in the car. I could feel her determination within myself. I could feel her absolute focus—her belief that nothing else mattered except what she was doing at that moment. "All of a sudden, as fast as though I had turned on a light," she said, "I was one with this pheasant. I was not Samantha anymore. I was this bird! I felt my wings deep down to their tips, and I flew! I felt the wind go through my feathers. I smelled the fresh air. I saw the large trees underneath me, as I gently flew above them. I saw the earth, the trees, bushes and flowers and a little part of a driveway. I don't remember seeing any streets. I flew with an ease, a naturalness. All my senses were wide open. Then I felt a hit and pain and fear and I opened my eyes. I was Samantha again."

My mouth dropped wide open. Wow! I would have loved to have an experience like that myself.

Samantha stopped for a moment, then continued, "As I opened my eyes, I saw the pheasant staring at me. He was only about two inches away. He looked at me as if I'd just told him the most fabulous, exciting story. He opened his wings and made the most remarkable sound. I felt the exhilarating sensation of flying in my own body as he flew past me, around the post, and out to the open side of our patio. Then he made a turn between the wall of our house and that of the neighbor's house, and disappeared into the sky. It took a long time before I could move. I was overwhelmed. Now I knew it was possible

to get information to animals. Only I had no idea how I'd done it."

"Do you know now how you can get this information?" I asked.

"Yes. Our thoughts are like living particles that fly around in the atmosphere. They originate in our individual mind, which is part of the group mind."

"Group mind?"

"Yes. For example, when you work together with other people, your mind along with the other minds create the group mind. On a broader scale, our thoughts are often picked up by others, which creates a mass mind. This is the mind of the masses of all people. Depending on how the mass of people feels, that determines what our experience will be. At the same time, if we personally feel more positive, if we give more love and joy, that influences the mass mind. So it is our responsibility. And then there is the universal mind. That is the mind of all living creatures and beings in this and other galaxies. And finally there is God's mind, which is the source of absolute wisdom and absolute love. Within these different minds, each of us gets information."

"You have to explain that to me a little bit more."

"Okay. Let's say you're sitting on an airplane and the airplane is flying into turbulence. Usually with the first strong shake, many people get frightened and think they're going to crash. Even if you individually don't have any fear about crashing, this same thought will come to your mind almost automatically. In this case, you're catching some of the group mind, because the thought was not originally yours."

What a concept. My thoughts are not my thoughts? "How do I know when my thoughts are mine and when they belong to someone else?" I asked.

"Well, you have to watch all your thoughts."

"Wow, I'm going to be busy with this one", I said to myself. Or did someone else think that? I was completely confused. Obviously Samantha could read this in my face because she started laughing. "Don't worry about it. Most of your thoughts are your own. But if a thought comes to you out of the blue that has nothing to do with you, take a closer look at it. After a couple of days you'll understand what I mean."

"I'm not so interested in the group thoughts," I admitted, thinking how wonderful it would be to think only divine thoughts. Wouldn't that also mean that all my questions would finally be answered? "How do I get to the divine thought group?" I asked.

"You can reach it when you tune into it."

"Like a radio?"

"Yes, something like that. First you ask for it. That's what I do with the prayer. Then you must believe that this is happening. You have to trust that the information that comes to you is divinely inspired, and you have to learn not to have any negative thoughts anymore."

I was familiar with this concept: Do not think any negative thoughts. Every negative thought keeps our wishes from being fulfilled. "You know how that works Sabrina, don't you?" Samantha asked.

"Yes, each negative thought is like a leash that pulls us back from our wishes."

"Exactly."

Some examples came to mind: *I would like to have some money, but I think people with money are all ignorant idiots.* The negative thought about people with money is the leash pulling us back. *I would love to find a great man, but*

I don't believe any great men exist. Again, that belief is the leash pulling us back. *I would like to make my hobby become my profession and make my living with my hobby, but I think that only exists in fairy tales.* Here again is our famous leash pulling us back from our dreams. "Also," I added, "if you want to talk to animals, it is very important to first believe that is possible."

"Oh yes, you can say that." She laughed. "If you have taken the first step, you want to take the next one. You open yourself in prayer, or in meditation, for the divine thoughts to enter."

"After Frosty was healed, did you begin a practice to use these talents?"

"You know, I always thought my mission was to help people as a healer and to teach them to heal themselves. I thought the healing of animals was the first step to prepare me for healing people. People were my clients, not animals. I thought of all the years I had spent studying about people and realized this experience would change my whole life."

I had to focus on my driving because we were leaving the freeway and entering the airport.

Samantha noticed my focus had shifted and waited until I had found the rental car return. As we lifted our luggage out of the trunk she continued, "I had a talk with my teacher. I sat before her and told her about the pheasant. I told her I could not work with people anymore. I had to learn and experience more about how to communicate with animals. 'That's wonderful,' she replied. 'It's time for you to meet the two angels who work with the kingdom of animals.'

"Sabrina, that was a great feeling. She spoke about *my* angels, the ones I'd felt since my earliest childhood. And she spoke about them as if everyone knew about them! For

the first time I felt validated. Here was someone who knew these two angels as well as I knew them! We meditated together and shortly after I closed my eyes I saw my two angels. They looked like a bright light that shone further than the physical form. I immediately remembered the curve of their wings. I felt the wonderful feeling of being taken care of that I had known so well as a child when my angels were close by. They spoke to me through this feeling, letting me know that what I was doing was right and that they would always be with me when I worked with animals."

"Did they tell you their names?"

"Yes, but I forgot the names. The feeling I will never forget."

"You know, I've never felt my angels that intensely. I've never had a feeling that they are standing directly behind me and if I looked up I would expect them to be there. Could I learn that?"

Samantha paused before she answered. "You know, Sabrina, I think it is a combination of a lot of things. First there is your commitment to God and your desire to do good things for people and, in my case, animals. And, of course, it helps to train your sensibility."

"How does one train one's sensibility?"

"You know, next week I'm giving another course about how to talk to animals and how important it is to trust your own receptivity. Why don't you join us?"

"I'd love to." I was thrilled with the invitation and could hardly wait until the following week.

80

Chapter Six

How to increase receptivity and where to find the point of happiness

A week later I drove down to Manhattan Beach, an area south of Los Angeles. Samantha's house was easy to find. On the door was a sign, "We honor the Japanese custom. Please remove shoes before entering."

As I took off my shoes, I was thankful for my white socks. I had barely gone through the doorway when something flew over my head. I bent down, jumped forward and almost stepped on a white rabbit.

"Come on in," I heard Samantha say from the kitchen. "I'm in here feeding Tootles."

Her husband Stan welcomed me with a strong hug and gently guided me into the kitchen. There was Samantha, tweezers in hand, feeding a creature without feathers that looked as though it had come from another planet. I laughed. I wouldn't have been surprised if Samantha were feeding an animal from another planet. Again I had the feeling we had known each other for a very long time. And, who knows, it was probably true.

"What happened to Tootles?" I wanted to know.

"I got him from a client. He has a weird disease. He lost almost all his feathers. He misses flying."

"And who are the guys who greeted me in the living room? The bird and the rabbit?" I asked.

"Hershey's in the living room?" Samantha sounded surprised. "Hershey, come in here!" she yelled into the living room.

A few seconds later, the little rabbit hopped around the corner. Tilting his head slightly to one side, he watched me carefully—or maybe that was just my imagination. At one end of the kitchen was a playpen with two additional rabbits in it. Looking out the window, I could see four cats eating their dinner. I noticed two nests on one of the kitchen chandeliers. I didn't see any bird cages. Obviously the birds were free to fly wherever they wanted.

"Aren't you worried the birds will fly away?" I was curious.

"I want them to fly away," Samantha said with a smile, "because that means they are healthy enough to take care of themselves."

I should have thought of that myself: of course, Samantha would treat animals as their own bosses.

Tootles finished his dinner and climbed onto Samantha's shoulder. He put his beak in her ear, then jumped over her back onto the floor. He waddled past the rabbit and made himself comfortable in one of Samantha's house slippers.

Samantha suggested we do a joint meditation and I nodded happily. On the way into her living room, I thought about how different my life was now. Four years ago, I would have gossiped with her about someone at the kitchen table. Now I prayed with my new friends.

I asked Samantha to guide the meditation. I'm always delighted to learn new meditation techniques and I wanted to know what she does in her own mind so I could try it as well.

We both sat cross-legged in the living room, our backs straight, our hands laid gently in our laps. "This meditation is one of my favorites," she explained in her soft voice. "It's so easy—all you do is listen to your breath."

Listen to my breath, that's all? Okay, I thought, I'm sure she knows what she's doing. I had no idea my breath made a noise. I took a deep breath in and a deep breath out. Yes, there was a sound. Then I breathed normally and, again, I heard this special sound. There was one sound when I breathed in and another sound when I breathed out. I focused on that sound and every other thought gently went away. I focused again and even the thoughts that were trying to come in disappeared. After a short time I noticed how peaceful and calm I was! This was probably the easiest meditation method I'd ever tried.

We had barely finished when we heard a knock at the door. I had to smile. The very moment we opened our eyes, there was a knock at the door! I thought how perfectly meditations always end. Isn't it fantastic how the Universe works?

Several people, barefoot or with socks, walked into Samantha's and Stan's living room. We introduced ourselves and Samantha's workshop began. First she asked each of us why we were there and what our animal's problems were. There was Michael, whose cat always peed in his bed when he went to the office. Olivia's dog scratched itself so badly he had bare spots on his legs. Karen's cat hadn't eaten since she'd moved. Paul's African Gray, a parrot, didn't want to talk. Linda's dog wanted to bite every other dog. And myself. My problem was my dog Sister, who loved Barney, our orange cat, and disliked Boots, our black cat. Every time poor Boots came into the house, Sister chased her out again.

Samantha nodded at all our explanations and stories. I had the feeling she'd heard them all before. Then she shared her story. She talked about how God was her father, her first

experience with the pheasant and the two angels who were always at her side. "Animals communicate through telepathy, which is the transfer of thoughts. But they do not transfer words, they transfer pictures," she said. We all listened carefully. "Have you ever noticed what happens to someone with a cat allergy when she comes into a home with cats?"

"Yes," answered Karen, whose cat didn't want to eat. "All the cats immediately surround her." We nodded our agreement. That was true.

"Why is that?" Michael wanted to know.

"What do you think this person is thinking about when she sees a cat?" Samantha asked.

Linda spoke first: "She thinks, 'Oh, my God, look at those cats! They're going to come right at me and then I'll have a terrible sneezing attack.'"

"Because she imagines this is what is going to happen. So she telepathically sends this picture, this thought," answered Samantha. "Then the cats feel they are being called for and they come."

"What should this person think?" Olivia asked.

"Exactly the opposite. You have to imagine the cats making a wide circle around you."

Of course, that was so logical. I'm always amazed when I hear such logic. I call it my "Ah-ha" experience that translates as: "Oh that's how that works!" And then: "Oh, I should have thought of that myself."

Samantha explained how we send telepathic thoughts to a person or animal. "First it is only when you feel love. You can't do it when you're angry or upset because no thoughts will reach the animal. An animal will pull back, just as we do, when somebody yells at us. Then you pray and you imagine in pictures—like a movie in your head—how you want the animal to behave. It's very, very important that you do not imagine what you don't like."

Ah-ha! So if I constantly imagined Sister chasing Boots out of the house, and if I said, "Don't do that," all Sister would receive would be the picture that Boots was supposed to be chased out of the house. Then that was exactly what Sister was going to do. Instead I had to imagine that Sister stayed quiet, even if Boots was in the house.

Samantha continued, "You also have to imagine how happy you're going to be when your animal does what you want. You have to send that feeling, too. Your feelings are like a telephone cable; they transport the pictures to the animal." Then she smiled. "But, of course, your animal still has the free will to choose if it wants to do you that favor or not."

We all laughed.

The sending of telepathic information seemed to be relatively easy, but what about the receiving of it? To teach us about that, Samantha asked us to pick a partner. I turned to Linda, a delicate thirty-year-old sitting next to me.

"One of you will send and one of you will receive," Samantha instructed us. "Decide who wants to do what and then close your eyes."

Linda wanted to receive first, so I agreed to send.

"In the middle of your brain center is a point of happiness. Imagine a straight line going from the point between your eyes and another straight line going from the center of the top of your head. Now imagine these two lines meeting somewhere in the middle of your brain."

In the middle of my head, I drew a vertical line going down and a horizontal line going inward from between my eyebrows. I followed them until they met. I found myself laughing, and heard Samantha say, "You'll notice you have to smile."

How does she know? I wondered.

"The person who is sending imagines a simple object with a very strong color. If the receiver believes he has an idea about the object, he says what it is."

What could I possibly imagine as the sender? Maybe a red ball. I hoped that would not be too difficult for Linda to figure out. So I imagined a red ball bouncing up and down; the red was strong and the ball like a soccer ball. I focused on the joy I felt playing with it. It was not easy to focus longer than five seconds on the ball—at least not for me. In the meantime, I suddenly saw an umbrella. Did I think of that by myself or did I catch someone else's thoughts? I went back to the ball. Then I remembered I shouldn't forget to write a note for my daughter Julia to bring to her kinder-garten teacher. "Sabrina," I scolded myself, "Why aren't you more focused?" And the red ball appeared again.

"I think it must be something round," Linda said.

Surprised, I opened my eyes.

Linda looked at me. "Is it round?" she repeated.

"Yes." I nodded.

"Maybe orange?"

"Almost." I tried to help her.

"Somehow this thing jumps. Is it a ball maybe?"

"Yes! You're great!" I was excited.

"But it's not orange?"

"Red—but, you know, orange-red!" I laughed. Wow, this was fantastic. I was thrilled. "Now let me try."

I closed my eyes and searched for the point of happiness, as Samantha had suggested. My inner vision was dark and I wondered what Linda could be thinking. "Stop it," I told myself. "Just wait for what's coming." I sensed a joyful expectation on the part of the others; maybe they had found their objects already. I was also aware that I was putting pressure on myself to succeed. Please dear God, I prayed, let me see, too.

Then out of nowhere a spoon emerged from the background of my mind. I opened my eyes. "A spoon," I said enthusiastically.

Linda looked at me with surprise and said hesitantly, "No, I'm very sorry."

I closed my eyes again. I saw hundreds of objects being thrown at me: an old car, a yellow dress, a little cat, a letter. This wasn't going to be easy. I thought I was probably the only idiot who couldn't figure out what the object was. By that point, I was completely distracted and could barely get back to the point of happiness.

I waited. What could she possible be thinking? My mind raced. It was like going on a scavenger hunt without the slightest hint. More objects were coming at me: a thick book, a ski, a candle. I was getting upset. I heard the others whispering with each other. Everybody had probably found their object, and I was the only one who hadn't gotten a clue yet. No wonder I couldn't see angels, if I couldn't even get an object telephathically. "Okay, try it again," I told myself. I decided to go to the point of happiness and wait for the next object that appeared—that would be the right one. I waited. It was a cow.

"A cow," I said, hoping this was the right one. I wanted to hear Linda say, "Sabrina, this is fabulous. You're absolutely right." I opened my eyes. I could see by Linda's expression that I was absolutely wrong.

"What is it, then ?" I asked in frustration.

"The sun!"

The sun! It couldn't get any easier than that. The sun was round, yellow and shiny. There was no connection between the sun and my cow. Maybe someone else nearby had thought about a cow and I just caught that. After all, what about the group mind? I inquired of the others. Nobody? Okay, very well then. I released a deep sigh.

We exchanged our experiences in the group. Except for Michael and me, everyone had found their objects.

"It doesn't matter," said Samantha. "It will happen."

The next task was to imagine a feeling and send it to our partner. Linda looked at me with reassurance.

But I'd had enough of receiving. "Do you mind if I send again?" I asked.

"Sure, go right ahead," Linda replied.

I closed my eyes and looked for the middle of my mind. I went to the point of happiness. Which feeling should I send her? I decided to send the feeling of loneliness that had been so commonplace in my life before. I felt as though I never belonged to anything. I played a role. I was on stage, an actress in my own life. I behaved as I thought others wanted me to behave. I felt how my stomach tightened up, my throat hurt me and my eyes burned. A part of me watched this feeling as a professor would watch something under a microscope. It felt as though a thick rope were connecting my stomach, my throat and my eyes. For the first time ever, I watched my feelings and didn't follow them. It was exciting to see how the feelings behaved and how I reacted. I felt the tears fighting for space behind my closed eyelids. I had almost forgotten how strong that feeling used to be. I took in a deep breath and opened my eyes.

I saw Linda had tears in her eyes. "Oh my God, this is so painful!" she said, and started to sob.

"Is everything all right?" I asked, startled.

"Wow! There is a feeling in my stomach as if everything tightened up and mushed together and I couldn't swallow anymore. It made me cry."

I stared at her with my mouth wide open. This was incredible! I nodded to every word she was saying. "How did it feel for you?" I wanted to know.

"You know I can't describe it in just one word." Linda closed her eyes again. "There was such a sadness, such a sense of being lost, such a loneliness."

My own eyes filled with tears. Yes, that was the feeling I was so used to and that I'd tried not to look at for so many years. We hugged each other. There was a closeness between us I'd never felt before with a complete stranger. There was a love and an honor, a shared understanding. It was wonderful, incredibly wonderful.

It was my turn again. With a deep sigh, I closed my eyes. I wondered how it was going to go. I went back to the point of happiness and heard Samantha say, "Just watch your body. Scan it from your toes up to see whether you notice a feeling or a movement that wasn't there before."

I tried that. My feet felt normal. My legs? Hmm, maybe a little heavy, a bit tired. Was that me or was it Linda? My stomach and heart area were normal. Throat, nothing. Mouth, also nothing. Oh, wait a minute. There was a funny stretching in my gums. I reminded myself to scan it without doing anything. My teeth felt as though they were pressed together. My jaw felt as if it had a muscle ache. It was a weird feeling I'd never felt before. As I concentrated on the sensation in my mouth and gums, I noticed an angry pulsation. The

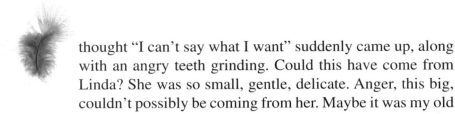

thought "I can't say what I want" suddenly came up, along with an angry teeth grinding. Could this have come from Linda? She was so small, gentle, delicate. Anger, this big, couldn't possibly be coming from her. Maybe it was my old anger.

"Come on, let's go. Open your eyes. This is taking far too long," I heard in my head.

"Be quiet!" I tried to calm the hectic part inside me. What I was experiencing was very exciting. This pain in my jaw was unbelievable. It was almost like a cramp. I opened my eyes and looked at Linda. I searched her face to see if there was anything written there that agreed with the feeling I had just witnessed. But there was nothing. She seemed perfectly calm. She raised her eyebrows and again I noticed how tender she was, like a little girl. Small shoulders, a light dress, her legs up on the couch. How could she be so angry?

"Don't worry about it, you're probably wrong again," I heard in my mind. Self-sabotage was always the most effective method to keep me from my own receptivity. Finally I found the courage to say, "I feel as if my mouth were in a huge, angry cramp."

I watched her reaction. Her eyes suddenly grew darker and she closed them. "Yes," she admitted sadly. "That was the feeling I had in my childhood. I always had to do exactly as I was told. If I didn't, I got hit."

Compassion came over me, like a wave. We hugged each other. It was as if we had been able to heal each other from our former wounds.

Later, as everyone said good-bye, Michael put it into words for all of us: "I'm leaving so much lighter than I came." We all nodded and laughed. It was true.

Still sitting in front of my altar, I thanked Samantha once more. I thought about what a wonderful woman she is. After I opened my eyes, I continued to sit for a little while.

It was amazing how quickly each of us had learned the first steps in telepathy. Obviously we all have this hidden talent. We just need to trust in it. It is a natural talent, like eating and drinking. But do we really want to be telepathic? I can't say to others, "This part of my brain is telepathic and I will allow you to read these thoughts, but this other part of my brain has little hidden secrets that are none of your business."

With telepathy there are no hidden secrets. There is nothing to hide from each other. There is only the clear, true "me." Of course, this would mean we would all be allowed to read each other's thoughts. What a concept! There would be no misunderstanding, no mistrust, no loneliness, no cheating—nothing like that anymore.

I contemplated this wonderful idea. We spend so much energy not showing the people with whom we live how we feel, that—with telepathy—we would probably all be much more relaxed. We could help each other without picking up the phone because we would feel if someone needed our love or our care. We wouldn't have to hide anymore, or pretend to be what we are not. I imagined the difference in our appointments and dates. Couples in love, married couples, parents, teachers, business people, politicians—all would get more done in one day than they now do in one year.

I have often found that people "accidentally" call me when I think of them. That is telepathy. Of course, it is just the beginner's level. I felt joyous about the future. All we have to do is be willing to let others read our thoughts. Maybe this is one reason wise teachers tell us to control our thoughts, to think positive thoughts. How many of my thoughts would I wish to have others read? Four years ago I would probably have said only ten percent. But in the last four years I have learned to watch very closely what I think. Now I would be comfortable with people knowing ninety-five percent of my thoughts.

But what about the leftover five percent?

When do I think these thoughts I might be ashamed of? Yes, when? Slowly they come to mind: When I judge people. When I criticize someone who is angry for not controlling his thoughts. When someone is dirty or sloppy. When someone blames everything on someone else.

And how do I get rid of these thoughts? I have to learn to have greater understanding for the people around me and for their different situations. When I have understanding, I do not judge so easily. Each person is simply looking to have love and caring and creativity in his life. I promised myself I would learn to concentrate even less on negative thoughts.

What kind of influence would it have on our angels if we all learned to control our thoughts and to communicate with telepathy? Wouldn't it be easier for them to communicate with us? I also wondered if the five percent of negative thoughts prevented me from seeing my angels. But then, why would other people who might not even control their thoughts as well as I did be able to see their angels?

I closed my eyes again, took a deep breath in and asked my angel: "Why do people who are not controlling their thoughts as well as I do see their angel?"

"Why do you think other people are not controlling their thoughts as well as you do? Isn't that an assumption?" I heard in my head.

Yes, that is true; it is an assumption. This must be something left over from my spiritual elitism. So I tried another approach: if we see angels in those phases of our lives when we think positively, wouldn't that mean children see more angels than do adults? I waited for the answer in my mind.

"From where do you think all these invisible friends of your children come?"

"Yes, but doesn't that mean they just have a very busy imagination?"

"Is that what you call it?"

"Are you telling me all the invisible friends of our children are angels?" I asked.

"Yes, that is what we are telling you."

How often I have smiled when parents told me about their children's experiences and thought what wonderful imaginations those children had. They were right. When we get older and accept our "reality," we lose the trust and belief and probably also the ability to see our angels. I have to talk with some of the children again. There is much to learn.

I stood up, went to my daughter's bedroom and leaned over her. She and I are always telepathically connected. So often she says something I have just thought about at that moment. I realized I needed to tell her about that more often so she knows what she is doing.

We became close friends, Samantha and I. I called her my sister. She gave me great hope. I learned so much from her. I learned that I can learn and grow, that belief and trust in our angels—even if we can't seen them—can change our lives.

Was it easier for Samantha to sense angels because she believed God was her father? Was it easier because she felt she was spiritual even as a little girl? Even as a child, she had special gifts. I didn't. I always had the feeling I had been switched at birth. I felt lonely in my family. The only spiritual moment I remembered from my childhood was the time I looked in the mirror and watched my face and said to myself, "That's how I look now. Isn't that funny?" Other than that, I only remembered having the strong feeling as a child that life must get better as I got older. I could hardly wait to live alone, to be my own person, to be an adult.

When I was a child, we lived under very trying circumstances. My father was very talented as a furniture upholsterer, but he found it impossible to deal with his finances. He was an alcoholic. In our tiny one-bedroom apartment, my mother shrank in her ability to live a joyful life. Three daughters, no help, no money. I saw her as a victim of my father. I had a clear idea about how beautiful family life could be. I wanted to create that for myself, but I knew I first needed to grow up.

On my twelfth birthday, I knew I had to go on for six more years! Six more years and I would have a space of my own. I felt it would be easier for me if I could live by myself and make my own choices. I didn't want to depend anymore on my father's mood. Six more years!

I would have loved to know about angels as a child, and to have felt them. I would have loved to have them comfort me. But, as far as I could remember, I had no experience as a child that even remotely resembled an angel experience.

Maybe it is a talent we are born with: that is, one person is talented in music, one in languages, another in seeing angels. Or perhaps seeing angels is something we can learn, as we learn reading or writing.

How important is it to see your angel? Is it not enough to just feel them? I tended to think I could speak with more authority, with more experience, if I had seen angels. Here I was giving workshops and seminars about how to make contact with the world of angels: wouldn't it be wonderful if I could say: "Yes, I've seen them with my own eyes; yes, I promise you they exist"? Wouldn't that help people understand what they were looking for when they came to my workshop? I would clearly be an expert. Was I less of an expert because I hadn't seen them yet? Hmm. I saw and sensed much more now than I had years ago. Maybe to see angels was just another step.

Four years ago I learned how to see an aura. It was easier than learning how to write. I read the book by James Redfield, *The Celestine Prophecy*, in which he describes how it works. The best time to see an aura is at the beginning of the sunrise or sunset when the light is not so bright. I couldn't wait until the sun set. Would I be able to see the aura of my finger? Would I be able to get my eyes to see something different? Would it be as easy as he described in the book? Would it work even if I were near-sighted? I was afraid it wouldn't work for me, or that I would just imagine it because I wanted to see it so badly.

Shortly after dinner I went outside. I took a deep breath to relax myself and said a short prayer. "Dear God, please help. I really want to see this aura!"

I lifted my hands to eye level about ten inches from my face, stretched out my fingers tips until they almost touched and focused on the tree in the background. At the same time, I tried to look at my fingers without focusing on them. In the book it said one cannot see an aura simply through concentration. Rather, there must be an easiness to it. Well, I found it was not so easy with this easiness to concentrate on what I wanted to see.

Wait a minute. Wasn't that a brightness around my fingertips? Automatically, I focused on them and it disappeared. Of course, that was because I was concentrating on my fingers.

I tried again, keeping my concentration on the background. All of a sudden I saw a very thin little shine around my fingers. Oh, wait a minute, it was getting larger! This was weird. I put my fingers down and glanced over the hills and background. Almost through "coincidence" I noticed that the tree was now in the foreground and I could see an aura around the tree. It was much larger than my finger and it pulsated. I was fascinated. I looked at the hills in the background and focused on the even darker sky behind. I noticed the whole hill had this shine around it. It was unbelievable. Why had I never noticed this before?

I went back to the house and screamed at the top of my lungs, "I can see an aura! I can see an aura!" The memory of this incident brought a smile. My poor husband had gone through so much with me already.

I stared at the candle flame that burned almost motionless on my altar. I could see the shine, the aura of the flame, a gentle light blue light that hugged the flame. I noticed little rainbow stripes when the flame moved suddenly. I had never noticed these before, probably because I had never really looked at them.

Maybe it was the same with our angels. Now I more frequently saw movements behind me for a few seconds or funny fragments when something was close by—for example, if someone passed by me or walked behind me. If I looked around however, it would vanish. Maybe that was an angel. Maybe I just had to gently, with easiness, watch this "something" that I could sense on the edge of my vision.

97

98

Chapter Seven
Why Angels like to help with everything and about the power of prayers

Because of my books, seminars, radio shows and articles in Germany I very often get mail, which I always answer thoroughly. I love morning time, as I walk from my altar to my desk, happy that my spirituality and my working life are so closely connected. My sanctuary is now also my office.

Years ago I'd been a closet believer. I didn't want to talk about my prayers. What would others think about me? I prayed alone if I wanted to pray. For example, if I sat down with a group of people to work on a project together, I never actively let them participate in my prayers. I prayed *for* them and not *with* them. I never included the whole group. I prayed with myself.

I noticed this habit for the first time when we moved. The house had everything we needed, but we wanted to renovate it. The only challenge was time. We didn't have much time for all the changes we needed to make. So this renovation would have to go differently than the one on our old house. Back then we spent double the money and five times the amount of time. Many problems occurred that I wanted to avoid this time. But how?

"Walk your talk," I heard in my meditations. I knew exactly what that meant. I had to do what I was talking about. Immediately I had an idea. I needed a prayer—one I could put on the front door of the house, so whoever came to work would know they were a part of this creation process and not just somebody who was paid to do his work. I had this thought and my angel Jao gave me a prayer. I wrote it down on a huge piece of paper and put it over the front door: "We request God's blessing for this land and this home. May all creation be done in joy and harmony and to the benefit and blessing of all people involved. Have a wonderful day."

I had Esther translate it into Spanish so the left side would be in English and the right in Spanish. An acquaintance of mine couldn't get over it. "But Sabrina, they must think you're crazy," she insisted.

I had to laugh. "Yes, and if I'm crazy, I can finally do whatever I want because I don't have to pretend I'm normal anymore!" What is normal? Normal changes in our society from day to day. One day this will be normal for all of us. I could hardly wait for it!

Then I met my contractor.

"Well, it'll take at least four months," was his prognosis.

"But I only have six weeks. Do you believe in miracles?"

"Miracles? Not in construction," he answered dryly.

"Look, I know that everything I believe and focus on is possible. I believe we can do this in six weeks and I have also made a plan for this. If you believe this is not possible, it will not happen because your belief will stop this project from happening in six weeks. So I can only hire you if you can bring yourself to believe it is possible to finish this in six weeks."

Pause.

Long pause.

He was thinking.

He was swallowing.

After a while he said, "Okay, I could give it a try. Maybe it is really possible to finish this in six weeks."

And we did finish it in six weeks. My angels supported me in every way. Each decision I made, I asked Spirit first. All predictions were correct. My workers got used to the idea of exchanging the word "problem" with the word "challenge."

One of my most fantastic experiences during this time was when the project manager Dave told me about a new challenge. He brought me to the back yard, to our terrace, that was laid in brick. One of the rain water pipes was clogged and they had been trying to push through that "challenge" but hadn't succeeded. Now they wanted to try to unclog it from the other side but they couldn't find the end of the pipe. Since we lived on a hill, the pipe could extend in almost any direction. They believed it went straight out and had spent the last seven hours digging at the end of the terrace. However, these pipes were only about five inches deep and one could easily miss them.

"What's the alternative?" I asked the three guys around me.

They told me they would probably have to break some of the bricks to find out where the water pipe was. If the pipe got clogged, they warned, it could back up into the house and cause a lot of damage.

"I don't want that," I said to myself.

I heard the thought in my head, "You can find the water."

"Me?"

"Yes."

"Okay, if you say I'm going to find the water, then I'm going to find the water."

I turned to Dave, my plumber and Daryl, the poor guy

who had been digging a hole at the end of the terrace for the last six hours. I said, "My angels tell me I can find this water pipe."

The plumber looked at me as if he needed to do emergency work in the plumbing department of my head.

A tiny voice in my head said, "And if you don't find this thing, you're going to be really embarrassed!" That was my fear, which was not as loud as it used to be, but occasionally still showed itself. Choosing not to focus on this thought, I walked to the point where the pipe started. I stood exactly on the spot where it began, closed my eyes and said my prayer: "Dear God, dear angels, here I am. I have no idea what to do, so you'd better help me."

I had a strong feeling I should keep my eyes closed so I could focus better. I also felt I should stretch out my arms. Then I had the strong feeling I would be pulled from the top of my fingers in the right direction. So I stretched out my arms and observed what I was feeling. The workers around me were very quiet and I could feel their curiosity.

"What should I feel?" I asked in my thoughts. I knew "feel" would be the only form of answer.

I scanned my body as I had learned from Samantha and I felt a very gentle pull in the top of my fingers. I moved slowly, with tiny steps, in the direction I felt the pull. One little step forward, then another little step forward. After a dozen steps I felt pulled to the left. So I took a little step to the left, and then another step to the left. Then I went ahead straight again. I took my little steps until I felt the hedge at the end of the terrace on my legs.

I opened my eyes and looked down behind this hedge. They had already dug there. But right where I looked down, right in the middle, no one had dug. There was a little leaf on the ground and I told Daryl: "This is where you have to dig. The pipe is under this leaf." I noticed the determination in my voice as I said this. I didn't say, "The pipe could be there." No, I said, "The pipe is there."

Dave and I went from the garden to the garage, which takes about thirty seconds. Immediately Daryl followed us with what was probably the most astounding expression of his entire career on his face. "We found the pipe!" He looked at me as if I'd just came from Mars. "It was exactly where you said."

I was happy about that. I'd never found water before.

"But you never searched for water, either," I heard in my head. That was also true.

Daryl came to me "Can I ask you a question?" he said a little hesitantly.

I nodded at him with a smile.

"Well, you know I've been watching you, the things you do and how you close your eyes and talk to your angels. But what I don't understand is that when I was I child I was told you should have respect for God and for your angels. I mean—" He stopped with an apologetic look. "You know, we shouldn't disturb God every five minutes because of something little. Don't our angels have something better to do than help us find water or walls or things like that?" His thought had finally come out and he took a deep breath.

"I understand what you mean. But do you have a relative whom you see every once in a while?"

He looked at me and I could see by his expression he had no clue why I was asking this question.

"Yah, I have an uncle I see every ten years at some family gathering."

"Would you say that you have a close relationship with him?"

"No, no, I wouldn't."

"Would you go to him if you needed help?"

"No, I hardly know the man."

"Well, that's exactly how it is with God and our angels. The more time you spend with them, the closer you get to know them and the better you can live with them."

"Okay, I can see that. But shouldn't we ask them only about the big things?"

"Why?"

"Don't they have anything better to do?"

"You know, maybe God and our angels are happy to be asked for help. Maybe then they feel invited into our life. And the more you invite them, the more they are a part of your life. It's like with relatives; the more often you invite them, the more natural it feels and the closer you will be."

"That's true."

"I believe it's very important to have a close and personal relationship with God. That way we live with our angels very normally, like close friends who are always with us. I, for example, even ask my angels for a parking space."

"For a parking space?"

"Yes. Every time I drive my car, I ask my angels for a parking space before I arrive."

"And?"

"I always find one."

"I'm going to try that, too!" He turned, around ready to leave, then stood there for a while, as if something else had entered his mind. "You know, I have another question."

"Yes?"

"Do we have to do something special to, you know, get our relationship with God and our angels a little ... more intimate?"

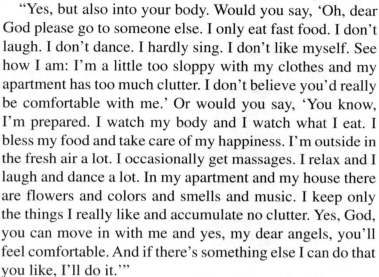

"Daryl, imagine God wanted to move in with you."

"What do you mean move in with me? Into my house?"

"Yes, but also into your body. Would you say, 'Oh, dear God please go to someone else. I only eat fast food. I don't laugh. I don't dance. I hardly sing. I don't like myself. See how I am: I'm a little too sloppy with my clothes and my apartment has too much clutter. I don't believe you'd really be comfortable with me.' Or would you say, 'You know, I'm prepared. I watch my body and I watch what I eat. I bless my food and take care of my happiness. I'm outside in the fresh air a lot. I occasionally get massages. I relax and I laugh and dance a lot. In my apartment and my house there are flowers and colors and smells and music. I keep only the things I really like and accumulate no clutter. Yes, God, you can move in with me and yes, my dear angels, you'll feel comfortable. And if there's something else I can do that you like, I'll do it.'"

He smiled at me. "I understand what you mean. We have to honor ourselves and take care of ourselves. Isn't that right?"

I nodded. "Yes, our body's our temple, our church, our castle, if you will. I understand this is God's body. And I'm renting it. At the end of my life I have to give it back to God." I laughed. "And I want my deposit back. It is my responsibility how this body looks and feels. That has nothing to do with vanity. It has to do with honor. And honoring yourself gives you the understanding to honor others."

Six weeks later the crew departed from my home. It had been a wonderful experience for me. It had taught me to trust the wisdom of my guardian angel even more in my daily life. It might be easy to be spiritual in prayer, but I saw I could also be spiritual in my daily life, even if that was

more challenging. When I trusted the messages I got from my angel, I had the trust I needed to overcome those challenges.

In my thoughts I thanked the crew who helped me create this space of working and praying that was my sanctuary, my studio. This room was the outer evidence that I did not distinguish between my spirituality and my normal life: I lead a spiritual life. That meant I showed myself to the world as I was. It was a challenge to bless my food even when no one else did so. Or not to gossip, even when everybody else was participating in it.. These were challenges for my honor and integrity. And sometimes I was a challenge for my family and the people around me. Was I how others wanted me to be? It was much easier to be myself.

I lit the candle on my desk next to the flowers. My desk had also become a sort of an altar, with crystals and angel statues, the candle that always burned when I worked and a bowl for incense next to my laptop. There was a statue of Joan of Arc and one of Einstein behind the pictures of my family. I liked to be surrounded by things that inspired me. I admired Joan of Arc for her strength to follow her visions against all odds and Einstein for his unconventional mind.

Then I opened the first letter.

Two hours later, my daughter Julia, still a little sleepy, came in and wanted to sit on my lap. We sang our 'Good Morning Song' and then went into the kitchen for breakfast. My husband Richard was sitting there reading his newspaper.

An hour later I kissed them both good-bye. Richard brings Julia to school every morning. I watched the car pull out of the driveway and then went to take my shower and get dressed. Afterward I met my assistant Sünje to discuss the current day: appointments with my clients, meetings, errands.

This morning my friend Deborah Renteria wanted to come by. She is a Jin Shin Jyutsu practitioner, which is similar to acupuncture but without needles. First she put her fingers on one's pulse and "listened" through her fingers to see how each organ felt. Then she gently put her fingertips on several acupressure points that create flows that balanced the body. When I had my first treatments with her, I didn't understand what happened to me. The only thing I knew was that it felt incredibly good. As I connected more and more with my body and better understood my physical makeup, I became more sensitive and learned to feel the flow of energy in my body. Then when Deborah put her fingers on parts of my body, I knew and felt exactly which organs or body parts connected to this flow. We had a mutual patient who'd recently had a cancer operation and we had planned this morning to meditate and pray for her.

The wonderful effect of prayers was proven to me by my Aunt Erna and my friend Stan. Aunt Erna was facing an operation and she felt the power of prayer on the day before she went in for surgery. "I feel so good, Sabrina," she told me on the phone. "So many people are thinking about me and I really do feel lighter because of that."

The operation was successful and after a week she was discharged. And with that the prayers stopped. After all, she was at home again. "You know, Sabrina, now that everyone thinks the worst is over, I don't feel their prayers anymore. They felt so good. I still need those prayers."

I understood. So her whole circle of friends and relatives started to pray again.

My friend Stan, a good-looking man in his middle sixties and a stabilizing force, had a heart attack. Instead of going

into the fear of dying, he used his will to focus on his desire to heal. This had not always been his philosophy. "Whenever someone was seriously ill, I could not stand to be more than a few minutes in that surrounding," he confessed to me. "I felt as if I couldn't breathe. I preferred to send flowers or write a thoughtful card or letter with my wish for them to heal quickly. I avoided funerals as much as I could. I even arranged a business trip to prevent me from going to one.

"I never wanted to admit it, but I was afraid to die. Every year I had a checkup with my doctor and he told me I was perfectly healthy. Then, one day, it hit me. As I left the gym, I noticed a funny muscle ache in both arms. The day before I'd been celebrating at a party, and I thought perhaps I'd drunk too much and had a hangover. I went home and my wife gave me a pain pill. I felt a little better and I wanted to go to the office. In the car I felt terrible, so I turned around and drove back home again. My wife noticed how gray my face was and we called a friend of mine who's a doctor. He listened to my symptoms for a couple of minutes and then sent me to the emergency room.

"In the hospital they ran all the possible tests until they found I needed a bypass operation because one of my arteries was eighty percent blocked. The operation was set for the next morning. On that day, my wife called all my friends and asked them to pray for me three times throughout the day. Some prayed alone and some prayed together. They all lit candles for me. After she spoke with all of them, I began to feel their prayers. Immediately I felt better. Within an hour, I was much calmer and more at peace. Before, I was very worried, nervous, anxious, angry and fearful. I, who always tried to avoid the concept of death as much as I could,

all of a sudden was facing an operation that could be life-threatening. Then a feeling of peace came over me.

"The operation was a success and my doctors told me they'd never seen anyone whose scars healed so quickly. I knew this had something to do with the prayers. If I hadn't experienced that myself, I would never have believed in the power of prayer. Quietness, peace, security, love—that's what I felt in me. Not bad?"

I asked him if he saw angels during that time.

"You know, Sabrina, I think it was a combination of prayers and the heavenly helpers. I didn't see any angels, but I felt hugged. The operation had a lot of blessings in itself. One of the greatest was that I'm not afraid of death anymore. I never thought I'd be in a crisis situation like that and act very heroically but, with the help of prayers, I mastered it very well."

Yes, everything is energy and no thoughts just disappear. Each thought reaches its goal. Each prayer goes to the one who needs it.

110

Chapter Eight

About Angels who are like heavenly aunts and about search, feel and trust

I could tell it was going to be a gorgeous day when I looked out the window. Most days in Los Angeles are sunny days. I could see Deborah's car parked in front of my house. I knew I needed Deborah's help again. Maybe she had some ideas about how I could continue my search for my angels.

From Deborah I had learned to listen to my instincts and also to talk about them. After taking my first steps into spirituality, I had been feeling very lonely. My long-time friends didn't speak about God, past lives or angels. My spiritual teachers were in Germany and I was all alone in L.A.. At least, that's what I thought back then. Now I know Los Angeles is one of the spiritual centers of the world and I have to laugh thinking about how lonely I felt on my path here in L.A..

In the months after my personal change, I started to notice that my friends were slowly disappearing. One after the other. Appointments were canceled, they moved or they were suddenly too busy. My husband also noticed this, which was cause for additional concern because he was already uncomfortable about all the recent changes. "You see," he remarked. "Maybe you're going a little bit too far."

I began to question myself. Maybe I was going too far. Wasn't there anyone here with whom I could talk?

Then I met Deborah at a party, and we connected immediately. She spoke about God the way other people spoke about dessert—in a very normal way. She said things like, "On a soul level, I think this or that," or "I have to meditate about that," or "I have a feeling of sadness" or "My angels told me to call you."

I didn't know anyone who spoke like that, who so openly discussed her feelings. I certainly didn't do it. Maybe others would think I was crazy. I wanted to be an intellectual. Back then I thought I had to choose between being an intellectual and being spiritual. Or I thought I had to turn off my mind and intelligence to find myself. My mind and intellect were perfectly fine, I later learned. I just couldn't let my intellect stop my feelings or let my intellect make all my decisions for me. My life was teamwork between God and me—my mind, my soul, my body and my heart with all its feelings.

I learned from Deborah to express myself. Not only the intellectual part of me, but the goddess part of me, the soul part of me and the feeling part of me. She showed me how and I learned fast.

"I have to ask you a question," I began as we sat outside in my backyard in comfortable garden chairs. We were sitting under a tree of orange-colored begonias. Deborah, who was in her forties and always joyous, picked up one of the fallen flowers from the begonia and touched it gently. "Tell me about your angels," I said. "Can you see them?"

"Oh, yes," she said and smiled. "Did I ever tell you how my angels taught me to swim?"

"No," I said. "Go ahead." I moved forward, curious to hear.

"Every summer my parents and I drove to the country-side where we had relatives. They had a house next to a lake and my parents were always a little concerned because I couldn't swim."

"How old were you?"

She pondered a moment. "I must have been five years old. My parents wanted to teach me how to swim as quickly as possible. They had been lifeguards—that's how they'd met. They were eager to teach me to swim because they loved the water so much," she explained with a smile. "But I was eager to teach myself. I just needed some quiet time to learn. One day my parents were up in the house and my father made me promise I wouldn't go near the lake. They were having some friends over and I was happy to have some time alone. I imagined I'd leave the adults without their knowing and go to the lake and try to swim by myself. I had my bathing suit on and I ran over and sat on the boat dock that goes out into the lake."

Deborah's eyes flashed excitement. "Finally it was time to try my skills at swimming. The guests arrived; there was coffee, tea and cake for them. The adults were so occupied with greeting one another that I quietly slipped away to the lake. I looked back at the house to make sure no was watching me. I ran to the end of the boat dock and looked at the quiet, empty lake. About ten feet from the pier was a boat gently rocking back and forth. It was a long canoe that was commonly used in this area for fishing."

"How long was it?" I was curious.

"About eighteen feet long and about four feet wide. It was made completely out of wood," she explained. "I stood on my tippy toes to make sure no one was in the boat, because sometimes the fishermen took little naps in there. But, no, it was empty. I was relieved because I wanted to be alone to learn how to swim. Sitting on the edge of the pier, I slowly moved my legs into the cool water. I held onto the pier with my hands. The lake was shallow and I could touch my feet to the bottom. The algae on the bottom moved through my toes and I sank deeper. I waited for a moment and then I noticed suddenly I wasn't alone."

"What do you mean?" I asked inquisitively.

"It was a feeling I can't describe very well," Deborah replied. Her eyes wandered up to the sky as if the answer were written there. "I had the feeling my heavenly aunts were around me. I definitely felt female energy. I heard high-pitched sounds, as if the angels were talking with each other. I couldn't understand what they were saying, but it sounded like incredible music."

Her eyes were shining as she shared this experience and I had the feeling she was reliving the moment. "You know, ever since I was a baby, I'd felt myself surrounded by angels. They'd been there for as long as I could remember. I always thought that having angels must be something very private because adults never talked about them. I felt lonely as a child," she continued. "My angels were my security. They were my heavenly aunts. Sometimes I saw outlines in light of my angels. It was always more than one. They were translucent, like frosted glass. They were shiny, and that was not just on the outside. My heart always felt joyous, the way it is when you see something very special to you. There was a feeling of deep remembrance. Almost like a feeling of being homesick. When you feel angels deep inside you, it's almost as if your soul wanted to dance."

She gave me one of her soft glances. Almost automatically I compared her angels experiences with mine. "So I was right," I said to myself. "She's not only felt her angels, she's seen them. And more than once."

Deborah continued, "As I was waist-deep in the lake, I heard my angels send me a quick 'No, no, no.' I remember that it came twice: 'No, no, no.' But I was so excited about learning how to swim that I didn't want to listen to their voices. I lifted my legs off the bottom of the lake, stretched them behind me and I threw myself, full of trust, into the water. As I expected, I was floating in the water. My lungs were full of air and I had my eyes closed and I merged with the feeling of the water. I loved to swim," Deborah remembered. "Not that I moved my arms or legs very much. I just enjoyed the quietness and I felt as if I were in another world. I slowly noticed that I needed to get some air. But as I tried to lift my head out of the water, I realized it wasn't possible. I felt a hard knock to my head and I became dizzy."

"What happened?"

"The movement of the water had carried me under the boat that was out on the lake. I was right underneath it and I couldn't get up. I opened my eyes to see what had happened, but the water was so muddy I couldn't even see my hands in front of my eyes. I stretched my legs down to find the bottom of the lake for support, but the lake was too deep in this area. There was only water under my feet. I thought I just had to keep going forward, but I realized I had practically no air left.

"Then, all of a sudden, I felt something on my left side. I turned my head that way and I heard a calming voice, as if someone were singing. 'Keep your mouth closed and leave your eyes open,' it said. I turned my head further to the left and saw something bright and shiny waiting for me. I couldn't see anything else in any other direction. Only there, on my left side, was this light. It was big. Everything moved in slow motion. This shiny ball attracted me like a magnet calling me to come to it. I knew instinctively I couldn't go straight ahead, as I'd first planned. I had to go the left. I had to go to this light.

"You know, Sabrina, I felt more than I saw. But I could actually see two shiny arms. It was as if a mother had stretched her arms out when her child was running to her. These arms were wide and outstretched and I knew automatically I had to swim to the left into these arms. I moved my legs a little and swam to the left to these open arms.

"The closer I came to these shiny, outstretched arms, the happier I became. There was a comforting presence awaiting me. I could barely wait to feel these arms." Deborah smiled at me as she continued, "And then I heard the high-pitched sound again. I knew instinctually I could lift my head out of the water. I remember how surprised I was that those arms didn't really catch me and pull me up. They were so clear and so strong and I felt so secure and so taken care of. I was so, so grateful that my body had been able to stay underwater for so long without any air. I was so thankful for my angels and my heavenly aunts. The light disappeared as soon as I had my head out of the water and filled my lungs with air. I found the fishing boat right next to me. My short, little kid's arms could barely grab the edge of the boat. But I grabbed it and held on."

"What would have happened if you'd swum straight ahead as you'd planned?" I asked.

"That boat was too long," she replied in a whisper. "I don't think I would have made it. My angels not only helped me with my swimming, but they also led me to safety and made sure I was healthy and alive."

"And your parents?" I wanted to know.

"You know, I never shared the experience with them. Back then no one talked about angels."

"What a wonderful experience." I sighed. Deborah watched me kindly. She knew me too well to not recognize there was something 'wrong' with me. "What's going on?" she wanted to know.

"You know, I really can't explain it well yet," I hesitated. "I have a feeling of ... failure inside. It's bugging me and it affects my mood and my comfort level."

"*You* feel like a failure?" Deborah laughed. "I don't know anybody who is as committed and focused as you are. You're famous for it. What other people do in a year, you do in a week."

Her compliment felt good. Yes, I acknowledged how fast and how focused I was. I have learned I do much better if I focus on one thing and one thing only. I used to do three things at the same time, but when I divided my concentration, I got less done. Now the more I concentrate my focus on one thing, the stronger the magnet. The stronger the magnet, the quicker my wishes get fulfilled. If I divide the power of a magnet into many little magnets, none of these magnets has the power to pull in what I want. Also, having learned to focus on one thing, in this moment, that focus is the angels. This is what I would like to take care of in one "famous" week.

Deborah watched me closely. "Where were you?" she wanted to know.

I sighed again. "You know, I notice how impatient I get. Shouldn't I be further ahead? Shouldn't I have seen my angels? Of course, I know everything comes at the right time and I have to let time happen. It's just so hard."

"Didn't you tell me that you wanted to write a book about angels?"

"Yes," I replied. "It will be called 'Loved by Angels.'"

"How far are you?"

"I haven't started yet."

"When is your deadline?"

"In three months."

"Well, no wonder you're a little impatient," she said dryly.

"You know, Deborah, first I thought I would just collect true angel stories from people I know and that would inspire other people to think about their angels."

"Well, that sounds good."

"But something is missing." I shook my head. "There is something I'm not seeing." My neck started to hurt me. "You see," I told Deborah as I massaged my neck, "my body reacts immediately when I talk about my doubts."

"What could be missing?" she asked.

"How can I write a book about angels if I haven't seen any myself? What a lousy expert I am. I just need more experience. What do you think?"

Deborah smiled. "You have experiences. Not in seeing them but in searching for them. You have experiences in trust and faith."

That was true. Maybe that was it. Maybe the search, the desire to see angels, the missing of it, the trust, the belief were my experiences. Wasn't that what connects us all, that desire to see them?

As I smiled at Deborah I felt again my deep gratitude for friends with whom I could talk about all these things. Deborah hugged me and said good-bye as I stayed behind on the patio with my thoughts.

Chapter Nine

How Angels help with healing and how they bring us from death to life

When do angels come and rescue someone in a life-threatening situation and when not? Is it when we would be shortening our life due to carelessness or because we are not "done" yet? Is it when we haven't finished our mission? Are some people more worthy to be rescued than others? No that couldn't be.

Once a woman asked a question about angels during my call-in radio show in Germany. She sounded very sad on the phone as she asked: "A girlfriend of mine recently died unexpectedly in a car accident. It was very painful for me. My six-year-old daughter noticed my sadness and asked me, 'Mom, where were her guardian angels? Why didn't they do anything?'"

I realized this was not only her daughter's question but also her own. She was hungering for a good explanation for herself, as well as one her daughter could understand. She was concerned that angels may only be mere observers instead of helpers during times when bodies had to be changed from one form to another.

I paused long enough to go inside and ask my angels to give me some helpful thoughts. They came up with the following wisdom: "Angels don't stop people from dying," I said to her. "When it is our time, then it is our time. But angels help us go from this reality to the next.

They are by our side. And after we've left the human body they greet us on the other side. Angels take away the fear of dying at the moment of death. It is like a caterpillar who becomes a butterfly. In between, when the caterpillar notices it has to leave its old familiar body to become a butterfly, there is a nervousness and an excitement before it opens its wings and takes its first flight. When we have this nervousness, angels show themselves. They help us with their love and give us the security and knowledge that we can, indeed, fly."

I heard a long sigh in my headphones. "Oh, that's how that is."

I felt this explanation had given her comfort. No, angels don't leave us alone when we need them most. They are by our side to comfort us. We just need to listen. Yes, listen, I said to myself. What about seeing? I had to laugh at my self-pity. But my understanding of dying and the part angels play in it is not yet complete.

My friend Teresa, who lived in Florida, worked in a hospital as a respiratory therapist. I had a strong feeling she would have insight into my questions: What do angels do when someone dies? What exactly is their job? What happens with the family and friends who are left behind? How and when do we feel comfort? In my mind I saw a picture of Teresa and had a strong desire to call her. I went back to the office and looked up her phone number. Let's see why I felt so compelled to call her. Wow, wait a minute? Couldn't I just ask my angel Jao about this? I closed my eyes to listen to the answer.

"Teresa has your answer."

Okay. I hoped she would be at home. I found her number and considered the three-hour time difference. Unfortunately,

I caught her answering machine. I left my phone number and a message, hoping she'd call back soon.

It was Sunday morning and, like every Sunday, I was looking forward to the group of women who came to my house between ten and twelve to meditate. We were a very loose group. Whoever had time and felt compelled to come, came. Every woman brought a stone the first time she came and held it during the entire meditation. At the conclusion of the meditation, she placed her stone in a circle with all the other stones that had accumulated. The stones stayed in this special place in my sanctuary all the time and greeted the various women as they returned to meditate the following week. If a woman was unable to personally make a meditation for awhile, she still received the energy through the stone that contained her unique vibration frequency.

It always fascinated me to see how the right group of women came every Sunday. Sometimes we were fifteen and sometimes only three. This Sunday we were nine women sitting on the carpeted floor of my sanctuary. There was a large bowl of water in the middle and around that about sixty stones and crystals left by the various women who had joined in the meditation. Next to the water was a bowl held by two small angel statues. Inside was a burning candle. Paula, a composer; Jessica and Ursula, two actresses; Monica, an art historian; Jenny, a music promoter; Deborah, whose angels taught her to swim; Connie, a broker; Sandra, a kindergarten teacher and Donna, an artist who paints angels, comprised the group on that day.

Connie was there for the first time, so I introduced her to everyone. We were sitting in a circle around the bowl of water encircled by the various stones and crystals and the burning candle. We held hands and Donna led our prayer. It was not a special prayer, just something that came into her mind. She smiled. Quietly and calmly she looked at everyone and closed her eyes. Her voice was sweet as she began, "Dear angels, beloved Light. We are here together to honor life and love and to support each other in the world. May we find this morning what we are searching for. May our questions be answered and may our bodies be stronger when we leave. Amen."

We hummed "Om" together until everyone had a feeling of peace and calmness inside. Then I led the meditation. As always, I listened to my inner voice and occasionally opened my eyes to see how everyone was doing. Sometimes tears or emotions came up and I wanted to be ready if anyone needed me during the meditation.

After the meditation, we shared our experiences using a talking stick. In the tradition of the Native American Indians, the one who was holding the stick could talk. She could talk as long as she needed to without anyone interrupting her. There was a wonderful advantage to this process. Those who were not sharing focused their concentration on the one who was.

Afterward we had a healing circle, and whoever needed healing placed herself in the middle of the circle. Each of us gave love so healing could take place. Our body has an unbelievable power to heal itself. Sometimes the only thing it needs is a little push to start the healing. Western medicine together with Eastern wisdom and with the understanding that disease is there to teach us about imbalance in our body or our soul is the ideal healing combination. Also, of course, it is important right from the beginning to give more thought to the balance of our soul and body so we don't need to get sick in the first place to receive attention. What we believe

about disease has a huge impact on our healing. A disease doesn't come to us like an engine failure in an old car. A disease comes to communicate something to us. It tries to teach us and to tell us sometimes that "enough is enough."

I'm hardly ever sick but a couple of months ago, I really came down with something. When friends asked me what was wrong with me, I'd reply, "I have a case of bad hearing."

The whole week beforehand, I was on my last reserves. I had done too much, pushed myself too hard. I was under pressure so I tried to walk barefoot outside as much as possible to fill up on energy. In meditation I heard Jao tell me, "Tomorrow you will spend the whole day in bed and you won't do anything. You must lie in front of the fire and just relax."

I knew how important this message was and that it was in my best interest to lie in bed. I listened to his advice and spent the whole next day in my bedroom, lying in front of the fireplace, letting the healing energy of the fire go into my field. I didn't talk with anyone. I prayed; I slept; I meditated. I watched the fire and felt peaceful. My assistant, Sünje wasn't surprised. She's used to my unusual life.

By 9 p.m. that evening I felt great. I was full of power and energy. My husband was away on a business trip and my daughter was in bed. Suddenly I remembered the thirty-five letters that needed to be answered. I went into my office, took my Dictaphone, gathered all the unanswered letters and made myself comfortable on my bed. I dictated and dictated and dictated. All my letters are very long and by midnight I noticed I'd answered a good half of them. But there was nothing left of the power and strength I'd felt some hours earlier. I was so exhausted I could barely move the letters and tape recorder to my husband's side of the bed. I crawled underneath the covers and started to meditate. I saw Jao in front of my inner eye. He looked at me and the only thing he said was, "Do you call that rest?"

Dumb, I said to myself. That wasn't helpful to anyone. Neither to my spirit nor my body. That moment, I noticed a sore throat that had not been there before and I started to cough. And, what a surprise, my nose was running again.

"If we say a day, we mean the whole day and you know that very well." That was the last thing I heard in my head. And then there was silence for the next three days. I was very sick for those three days and I blamed myself for it. I was in bed for three days instead of one. As I admitted, when asked, I had "a case of bad hearing."

It is always wonderful to see one of our sisters lying in the middle of our Sunday meditation circle, enjoying complete relaxation, as if she were taking an energy bath. She feels cared for, protected and surrounded by sisterly love.

This Sunday it was my friend Donna Terody, a painter, who needed help. Her ovaries were acting up. She had been sexually abused by her father and this memory has been stored in her ovaries. She is petite and delicate and usually dresses in white. Her long, light red hair is braided.

I dipped my hands in the bowl of water, moved them over the lit candle and united myself with the elements that create us. Then I moved my hands with the palms facing down over her body. Connie who had been here for the first time watched what I was doing with curiosity, so I explained to her the power of love. "I believe that many diseases could be healed if we just held the ill person for days and days."

More scientists are finding out how important it is for people to help one another. For example, New Jersey's Co-

lumbia Presbyterian Medical Center now has healers in their operation room. One of the leading heart specialists, Dr. Mehmeth Oz, has healers stand at the head of the operating table during an operation to balance the energies. You can imagine how brave this doctor is. Another leading heart specialist, Dr. Dean Ornish, considers meditation to be one of the leading factors in avoiding a heart attack. There are now insurance companies that reimburse for healing programs that include meditation.

Donna lay in the middle of the circle with her eyes closed and we all sat around her. "Connie, put your open palms down and place them about three feet from Donna's body." Connie moved a little closer, lifted her arms and stretched them above Donna's body.

"Now move your open hands slowly downward. All of a sudden, you will feel feel some kind of resistance." I nodded to her. "Go ahead."

Connie closed her eyes and concentrated as she slowly let her arms go from three feet to two feet, from two feet to one foot above Donna's body. Then she stopped and said, "There, there." She was surprised. "I feel the resistance." She opened her eyes. "What was that?"

"That's Donna's aura, the energy field around her body. You can measure it, and even photograph it. You know, we don't stop at the skin; we're much larger than our body."

Connie looked at me with surprise. "Do I have that, too?"

"Of course. We all have it. Each object, each stone, each tree, everybody."

"Why?"

"It's our sensory field, where we gather information. For example, hasn't it happened, as you walk into a room of people, that you feel immediately uncomfortable?"

"Yes," replied Connie. "Just last week I was at a terrible party and I felt very uncomfortable."

I nodded. "That was the vibration. You felt the vibration, the sensory fields of the other people there. We not only take in information with our eyes, ears and nose, but also with this sensory field, this aura. When your sensory field touches other sensory fields, your soul touches other souls. You're filled immediately with information, even before you say the first hello."

Connie drew her hands back.

"No, wait," I said. "Stretch them out again."

She stretched them out.

"Close your eyes."

She closed her eyes.

"When someone is sick," I continued, "the body is not in perfect balance. But it is seeking balance, a more perfect harmony. When do we feel most in harmony and in balance?"

Connie thought a moment. "Well, when we're comfortable. When we love someone or feel loved. When we're with friends and feeling joyful."

"Exactly. Then our sensory field is full of positive charge. If the body is happy and the soul is at peace, the sensory field pulsates with the most beautiful colors." I paused, then added, "Connie, say a prayer to God and ask for his assistance. Then go back to a time in your life when you were completely happy."

Connie was quiet, her eyes closed. "I've got it," she said after awhile. She was smiling happily.

"Now imagine this feeling going all through your body." We all watched as Connie began to smile more broadly. "Now feel the love coming out of all your pores."

Connie nodded.

"It also comes out of the center of your palms."

Connie nodded again. Her open palms were still stretched out over Donna's body.

After awhile I asked quietly, "How do you feel, Donna?"

"Wonderful. Connie's hand feels very warm. I feel much lighter now."

"Really?" Connie looked at Donna in surprise. "I didn't know I was a healer."

"Isn't that fantastic? Everyone is a healer." I smiled. "We just have to start healing."

Then all the other sisters moved their hands over Donna, sending her love. Jessica felt inspired to hold Donna's feet. I felt inspired to blow my love for Donna into her heart. The breath holds the power of our love and our life-force. Donna enjoyed the love and tenderness we were giving her.

Jessica was next. "It's very busy at home these days. I could use a little peacefulness," she said.

Two of the women gently stroked her arms. One held her hands and I held her feet, while two more moved their open hands over her body. She took a deep breath and someone said, "God, are you beautiful!"

We all started to laugh.

"You know what is most wonderful about this?" Paula remarked. "I can caress a woman's arm without someone thinking I'm a lesbian."

We all knew what she meant. She wasn't being judgmental about homosexual love. If that was what made someone happy, that was wonderful. But we could all remember times we had stopped hugging another woman because deep inside we were afraid someone might think we wanted something. We were sisters, and sisters hug each other; they hold each other and take care of each other.

My girlfriend Rita once explained to me that, when I conduct a pipe ceremony, I look like a man. And that's true. The pipe ceremony brings out the male side of me. If I dance or heal, more of my feminine side comes forward. All of us are both male and female.

As always, the two hours passed very quickly. "Thank you, ladies," Jessica said smiling.

We hugged her. Then I shared a question I had: "As you know, I'm writing a book about angels and I still need some angel experiences."

Deborah said, "I shared mine with you."

Donna picked up her handbag and said, "Well, I can tell you about the angel who came to me when I died."

Everybody stopped what they were doing and stared at Donna. "You died?" asked Paula.

"Yes," Donna replied in a matter of fact way.

"This I want to hear," remarked Jenny as she sat back down. "I'll make time for this story."

We all sat down again and Donna began, "I was on a sailboat when I had the most terrible kidney pain of my life. I noticed that I left my body—"

"Wait a minute," I interrupted her. "I need the beginning of your story. When did you first have contact with angels?"

Donna didn't have to think for a second. "I was four years old. My father was, as always, terribly upset and angry. He hit me and screamed how useless and stupid I was and that I was just in the way. Thank God, my grandmother came by to take me to a museum. I was able to leave the house and my father's wrath of judgment.

"In the museum, I saw a painting by Goya hanging on the wall. It had a little boy in it. I heard a strange voice in my head tell me I'd be a painter one day. I knew this was

God's voice. I felt much better after I heard that. From that day on, I started to paint regularly. My father constantly told me it was useless and I would only waste my time and his money."

"What about your mother?" asked Connie.

"My mother always pretended not to notice anything."

"Even when he hit you?" asked Connie again.

"She left the room then."

We stared at her with our mouths wide open. "Did your father ever hit your mother?" asked Paula.

"No, my Mom would have left him. So he took out all his anger on me. I believe now that he had a split personality. I never knew what would trigger his fits. It was completely unexpected, so I was always nervous and afraid. I thought constantly about killing myself. I had chronic pain in my abdomen. Only a couple of years ago the memory came back that he had molested me from age five to nine. I had completely suppressed this memory. When I was about eighteen years old, my father became very ill. My mother told me it was all my fault. If I hadn't made him angry so often he wouldn't be in the hospital."

Donna glanced at her hands, then said, "She said it was entirely my fault. For eighteen years of my life I was told how stupid and dumb and useless I was and somehow I came to a point that I believed it. I was never praised for any talent I had, so I never thought I had any. When I was eighteen years old, I felt I had nothing worth living for. I locked myself in the bathroom with a huge kitchen knife and I was going to cut my throat."

Deborah took Donna's hand. Donna smiled at her and continued, "As I took the knife and put it to my throat, I saw myself in the bathroom mirror and heard the same voice

that came to me in the museum when I was four years old. I heard, 'It's not you. It's them. Don't you see that? You have to understand that your family is sick. You're completely normal.'" Donna swallowed hard.

"This was such a relief to me. People who've never been physically or emotionally abused don't understand what it feels like. If you're always told as a child that you're useless, and if you're never praised for anything; if you've never felt motherly or fatherly love and hugs, you believe you are worthless. At some point you can't take it any longer."

"What did you do?" Monica wanted to know.

"I left home in the middle of the night. I was terrified my father would catch me and bring me back. Because of the voice in the bathroom I felt stronger. Something in me woke up. I decided I'd go to the police if my father touched me one more time. I spent the night with a fellow student from the fashion institute where I was studying. I needed some time to think about what I should do and where I should live.

"On that same day, one of my teachers talked with me. I was wearing an outfit I had designed and sewn myself. I think she realized what rough shape I was in. I'd never told anyone about the situation in my household. This teacher told me she believed the clothes I had created were marketable and she gave me names of different stores. She suggested I find out if anyone was interested in buying some of my clothes. I did that the next day and each of the stores ordered something. That's when I started my designer career."

We all took a breath of relief and thanked God that her terrible childhood was over.

"Some years later I met my husband Peter. Not only did he meditate, but he was very romantic—flowers, limousines, first-class travel, only the best hotels. He really spoiled me. He made a lot of money in the stock market and he inspired me to paint again. At first I believed he was genuinely concerned about me; only much later did I realize he simply wanted to control me. As a child, his mother had given him to an orphanage and he lived with the constant fear that he would be left alone again. He believed the more he controlled me, the more likely I would stay with him."

"How long were you happy with this man?" I wanted to know.

"The first year was fantastic. We moved to Australia and had a wonderful time there. A year later he sold his business and we moved to New York. After awhile he stopped working and spent all his time with me. I soon found this was a little boring. I wanted to paint. Then our problems started. I was beginning to sell some of my paintings and newspapers printed reviews of my work. I created with abstract forms and mirrors and I began to prepare for my first huge show.

"Our home was like a hotel, so many people were always around. Peter's almost grown son lived with us, as did a friend of mine who was broke. Then there were two assistants who worked with me on my show, the people from the gallery and a PR woman. As the day of my gallery opening approached, I had hardly a spare moment for my husband. My girlfriend who lived with us offered to take care of him.

"Peter became obsessed with the idea that I would soon leave. I had a body guard, a limousine with a driver and my husband always knew exactly where I was so he could reach me at any time."

"Absolute control," Paula remarked dryly.

Donna nodded. "In the meantime, my girlfriend put the moves on my husband. Everything was a complete disaster.

One time I returned home late at night without my key. I rang and rang and rang but Peter wouldn't let me in. He pretended he didn't hear me. I had to spend the night in the car because I never had much money with me. He wanted to teach me a lesson that I shouldn't come home late at

night."

"Did you leave him?" asked Jessica.

"No. I still loved him. A couple of weeks later was the opening of my show and everything was supposed to be perfect. I had great PR and everyone loved my paintings. But no one bought them."

"Why not?"

"My husband insisted on pricing the paintings. He priced them far too high. I wasn't a famous artist, I was still at the beginning of my career. I tried to explain to him that the art market doesn't work that way. But he assured me he was a successful businessman, he earned millions and he knew what he was doing."

Donna shook her shoulders. "You know, back then, I wasn't self-sufficient enough to trust myself. I believed I didn't have any choice. Thank God, I've learned a lot since then. We lost all the money we'd put into this gallery opening. Peter was angry and upset and it started a chain of bad things. One business after the other of his went broke. And then I started to get sick. The kidney problems that had bothered me since childhood became worse and almost took my life. We had to sell everything. The only thing left was a fifty-three-foot yacht in the Bahamas. So we went to live on this boat."

"You lost everything else?" I asked.

"Almost everything." Her voice grew softer and her eyes searched the ceiling as if something she wanted to share was written up there. "It was a Thursday the day I died. I remember it clearly. There was a bad weather storm warning but Peter wanted to sail out into the ocean anyway. I lay on the couch, too weak to protest effectively. I had an incredible pain in my kidney and I had the feeling Peter wanted to kill us both out there because he was convinced I would leave him soon. Who knows.

"The storm came and it was the most terrible storm I'd ever experienced. At the middle of the day it was as dark as night. The waves crashed with incredible power on the deck of the boat. It thundered and lightning flashed and the yacht rocked so violently I had to lie down on the floor because I couldn't hold myself on top of the couch anymore. Peter stared at me. He was as white as the wall and I screamed at him through the noise of the storm, 'I hope you're ready to die. I'm going to start praying.'

I believe it was at this moment he realized what he'd done. He screamed, 'Oh, God! Oh, God! I'm not ready to die.'

It seemed the storm, the thunder would never stop. But, somehow, after what seemed like days, we survived. The storm had pushed us back toward the shore and Peter swam to get us food and a new dinghy because ours had gotten lost in the storm."

"How were you doing?" Jessica asked.

"I'd never felt so bad in my life. My whole body was in excruciating pain. Each muscle was in a spasm. I had the most terrible migraine and tears ran down my cheeks. I was thirty years old and I'd had terrible migraines since I was four. I was tired. My marriage was a catastrophe. I couldn't afford to buy the easels for my paintings; we couldn't even afford to rent a flat to live. I told God I was done with this life; I didn't want to suffer anymore."

Donna took one of the pillows and put it in front of her stomach.

"Then suddenly I felt as if I were being sucked out of my body with a huge vacuum cleaner. I saw an incredible white light. I was sucked above into it. I had no control. I was in the middle of this wonderful light and I didn't even remember who I was or what my name was. I looked around and saw figures who seemed to be made out of this bright light. They were looking down on me. As I glanced down at myself, I noticed I looked like them. I felt so peaceful. It was the first time in my life I'd felt this peace inside. The first time in my thirty years of life! I thought of nothing. I was just there.

"Then I realized I was moving slowly downward. I remembered again who I was. I saw the yacht from above and I saw Peter in this little dinghy as he rowed toward our yacht. In the next moment I was inside the cabin again and I saw myself lying down. My lips were blue and my face was white as the wall and I knew I was dead. I had seen my father die and he had looked exactly as I looked."

"How did you feel?" asked Paula.

"I was surprised that I didn't care about my body anymore. It was completely uninteresting to me that I was dead. I was a little concerned about Peter and what he would do if he found me this way, but I pushed that thought far away from me. I wanted to go back to the light. I tried, but I couldn't move upward anymore. One second later I felt I was going back into my body and all of a sudden I was there, in me, again. I opened my eyes and I saw a huge angel above me."

"Describe it to us," said Donna.

"It was huge. Our cabin was about nine feet high and the angel must have been fifteen feet high. I wondered how he fit into this little cabin. He was hovering above me and an incredible light surrounded his body."

"Any special colors?"

"No, I don't really remember how he looked. I just remember he was huge. He felt very masculine. I remember that. I was angry. I didn't want to be in my body. I told him I wanted to go back into the light, but I didn't get any answer. After a while he disappeared."

"And you were alive again?"

"Yes." Donna nodded. "I had no idea how much this experience would change my life. Almost all my pain was gone. My migraine never came back and even my kidneys were healed. I started to paint again. I painted an angel with a baby in her arms. Then I left my husband and went to Los Angeles. I started painting only angels. There is a window to the angelic realm, a different world opening up to me. This new reality inspired me to make better choices Since then, people began to collect my angel paintings."

"Two of the paintings in my sanctuary are Donna's." I pointed to the wall where they hung.

"Oh, I noticed them as I walked in. They're beautiful," said Connie.

"Thank you," replied Donna.

"I know you talk a lot with angels. How did you start?" I asked.

"It started with a hum in my ear. Almost as if I'd been flying in an airplane and my ears had become plugged. First I went from one ear doctor to the other, but no one could find anything wrong. Then I noticed that my angel talked to me that way."

"How?"

"Once in a while I would have a sharp pain in my ear.

After awhile I started to watch when I would get these pains."

"Really?" Jenny was curious. "Sometimes I have a hum in my ear."

Donna looked at Jenny. "Whenever the people around me were lying, I would get this little pain."

"That's fascinating," said Jenny. "I have to watch when I hear these noises and when I feel these pains."

"Yes. All of a sudden I had a warning system, a built in warning system and that helped me in a lot of situations."

Paula had another question. "Once I had the feeling that a huge vacuum cleaner sucked me out of my body. I was terrified. But through my will power I was able to stand up. I never thought I would die if I surrendered to it."

"You know, I know this feeling too," I said. "It happens sometimes and then I suddenly move to a different reality. That happens a lot without feeling I'm dying. In the beginning, I was afraid, but only because it was new and no one had told me about this kind of experience. I had no idea what was happening. Now I actually look forward to it. I also noticed I can come back into my body any time I please."

"How?"

"I just say, 'I am a child of God.' Since I don't know my way in this other world very well, the sentence, 'I am a child of God' is basically my travel guide. If I want to go home to my body I say, 'I am a child of God and I want to go back into my old body' and the next second I'm back in."

"Donna, I have to admit I'm confused." Connie leaned forward. "How did you know you were dead. Maybe you just imagined all this. Don't get me wrong." She looked concerned. "It's not that I don't believe you. I've just never met anyone who ... who ... died before." She laughed nervously.

Donna smiled tenderly. "You're absolutely right that this is very unusual and I completely understand your doubts. You know, it's hard to explain. I just know with a thousand percent this happened and I was dead. This experience was real." She was quiet for a moment, searching for a better explanation. "When did you have your first orgasm?" she asked Connie.

"Excuse me?" Connie was laughing. "Well, I guess I was about twenty-four or so."

Donna was grinning. "Before you had an orgasm, did you ever question what it would be like? When you had one, did you doubt that's what it was?"

"Okay," Connie admitted. "That's right. If I had a fairly decent experience, I thought maybe that was an orgasm."

"And after you had your first orgasm at age twenty-four, how was it then?"

"Well, from then on I was completely sure."

"See, it's the same when you die. Once you've died, you're completely certain about it."

We all laughed. Connie was laughing so hard she was practically rolling on the floor. And, to think, I once thought spiritual people were boring!

138

Chapter Ten

How Angels console you if you leave one body and get another

My friends were leaving. My daughter Julia who just walked into my studio blew out all the candles. As I got ready to leave my sanctuary, I glanced at the answering machine next to my desk. The light was blinking, so I pressed the message button. I heard Teresa's voice, my friend from Florida. "Hello, Sabrina, this is Teresa. It's Saturday evening. You can reach me tomorrow morning; I'll be here until noon."

"How wonderful," I said to myself. "Isn't it fabulous how easy everything is going again?" I thanked my angel and asked my daughter for a little more patience. I turned on my computer.

"Can I stay here?" asked Julia.

"Of course, my darling."

Julia went to her altar and started to rearrange it. She was looking for the perfect place to put the special stone she'd found yesterday. I sat on the floor in front of my low desk and dialed Teresa's number.

"Yes, this is Teresa," I heard on the phone.

"Hi, it's me, Sabrina."

"How are you? Nice to hear your voice."

"I'm doing great, thank you very much. Teresa, I'm writing my book about angels, and you've been constantly coming into my mind."

I heard her laugh on the other end of the line. "Isn't it amazing how that works?"

"Yes. You know, I'm trying to answer the question: 'What do angels do when someone is passing?' Have you perhaps had some experiences with this in your profession as a respiratory therapist?"

I heard her swallow on the other end of the line. "Yes. Last month."

"Could I share it in my book?"

"Yes, of course."

I moved the phone closer to my computer and asked, "Do you mind if I write the details in my computer as you tell them to me?"

"Depends how fast you are!" she replied.

"Fast," I assured her. "I'm ready."

"Now let's see, it was a while ago, but I remember it happened on a Monday. I was in the hospital working. The whole day I felt very funny."

"Were you sick?" I asked, as I typed her answer in my computer.

"No, not really. I just had a feeling I should go home as soon as possible. I felt restless, and that I needed to leave. I told my boss I wasn't feeling well and she sent me home. I was relieved I could finally leave. I was in a hurry, as if I were about to miss an appointment. I took my car out of the garage and drove on the two-lane highway home."

"Did you feel better?"

"Yes, but I still felt restless. I soon found out why. I'd been on the highway barely ten minutes, driving about fifty miles an hour, when the car in front of me suddenly stopped short and moved to exit to the right. He had recognized the exit at the last moment. I slammed on my brakes and, thank God, there was enough distance between him and me.

"Then I heard wheels screech behind me. I looked in the rear view mirror and saw that the person in the car behind me had lost control. That car headed left into the south-bound traffic. It happened very quickly. I saw the car slide past me and heard a horn blowing on a huge truck coming from the other side of the road.

"My heart almost stopped. The truck driver tried to brake, but he was too late. He crashed into the car's passenger side, propelling it into the bushes on the side of the road. It turned and twisted several times and came to a stop after about three hundred feet."

I felt an incredible sadness well up inside.

She swallowed. "It was unbelievable. I stopped my car on the side of the road and ran across to the accident. Some other cars also stopped and everyone ran to the scene of the accident. Then I heard someone scream, 'There's a baby in the car.' The driver was a woman and her car seat was bro-ken in half. She had fallen backward and half her body was hanging out the back window. Her legs were in the back seat, and her upper body was leaning out. The whole car was crushed and some people were attempting to pull the unconscious woman out through the window."

"I went to the front passenger side. There was a ten-year-old boy in the front seat and a baby in the child seat in the rear. All the doors were jammed and we couldn't open them. I screamed, 'We need to get the kids out!'

"A man brought his huge tool box and tried to break open the lock. The back window behind the baby was shattered but no one could reach through it. I stretched my arm through the front passenger window trying to reach the baby.

The broken window scratched my skin and I started to bleed."

"Was there blood anywhere else?" I asked.

"No, nowhere. As best I could, I stretched my arm to the back and reached the baby's wrist with my fingertips. Finally I found the spot to check his pulse. I prayed and I prayed I would feel one." Teresa's voice started to get softer. "But there was no pulse anymore. The baby's lips were blue and his face was so terribly white. I couldn't get close enough to give mouth-to-mouth resuscitation."

We were both quiet for a while.

Then I heard Teresa take a deep breath. "The ten-year-old boy was still breathing, but I couldn't get close enough to him to check him out further. Five minutes later the ambulance came, but they were too late. Both children were dead."

I felt a deep sadness in me. I looked at my daughter who was playing at her altar. How terrible it must be to lose your child. It would be like losing part of yourself.

"The police came and put screens up to provide privacy for the accident victims," she continued. "The people from the ambulance tried to get the mother out of the car. Occasionally she regained conscious and then she screamed in pain. I don't think she knew her children had died. She went in and out of consciousness. I felt completely exhausted as I stood next to the car. I cried and prayed; prayed and cried.

"Then it started to rain. You know how storms are here in Florida. It rains almost every day and, when it does, it comes quickly and in buckets. Only ten minutes had passed since the accident. I looked at the squished car and I prayed for the mother and her children. As a witness, I had to remain at the scene to give the police my statement. I was soaked by then, so I went to wait in my car. I closed my eyes. Suddenly I saw angels."

"Where?"

"Right next to the passenger side. Then I saw the children. The angels had made a circle around the children."

"How many angels did you see?"

"There must have been about fifteen to twenty. They were shiny and beautiful and huge. Their wings were stretched out so the kids couldn't see the car or their mother. I felt I had been given permission to see the children in the circle. The children were laughing and enjoying flying. The whole scene happened about six feet above the ground. You know, it seemed to me that the angels tried to distract the children so they wouldn't have to look at the accident scene again. I had the feeling that if the children chose, they could focus on the accident and see everything again. But they were too busy playing with the angels."

"How old was the baby?"

"He must have been nine or ten months old. I also had the feeling that the baby was there to help the ten-year-old boy with this experience. The baby, of course, had a more vivid memory of his time before birth because he was so young. The older we get, the more we forget about the time before our birth. The baby moved much more naturally in this new environment. In my head, the thought formed that the ten-year-old boy had made this arrangement with his little brother before his birth, so they could go together and the little brother could help the big brother."

"How long did you see the angels?"

"I don't know. There was no time for me. After awhile I lost the angels from my view. They became translucent again and, with them, the souls of the children. They faded away like the end of a movie scene."

"Where was the mother?"

"She was still in the car. I stood there for another hour until they got her out of the car. I had the feeling I was there to help the mother. Of course, you know how our sensory field works. I imagined that mine got larger and larger and touched her sensory field so I could send her my love and comforting thoughts. The police wanted me to tell them how the accident had happened. I asked if they could wait because I wanted to pray for this woman."

"Did the police accept that?"

"Yes. The policeman smiled sadly at me and nodded. 'I understand,' he said. Finally the woman was removed from the car and the ambulance drove her to the hospital. I waited in the car for the police to return. I wanted to meditate to see if the children were still all right."

"How did you do that?"

"I took about two or three deep breaths and asked in a prayer if there was anything I could do to support the mother and the souls of the children. Then the top of my head opened. As in a movie, I saw other dimensions. I saw the children still with their angels. I knew immediately they were fine. I felt their peace within me and their joy that they could fly again. I came back into my body as if I had been caught by a lasso when the policeman knocked on my car window. That was it."

"What an experience! How do you feel the mother is doing now?"

"I often feel her pain. She feels guilty about the death of her children. I was never able to make contact with her. I believe it is important she knows her children are safe and

happy. I would like to share with her what I saw. Perhaps it would help her to heal. It is my prayer that she will get the message from the angels through your book."

"Oh yes, I wish that for her with all my heart! I'll keep her in my prayers."

"Thank you," Teresa replied. "See you soon."

My neck was a little stiff as I placed the receiver back on the phone. I wished very much that the mother in Florida would find comfort in the thought that her children were still "alive." This life is different from the life we know here on earth. And missing those who are gone can be the hardest part. You can't touch them anymore. You can't hear them anymore. And often you weren't even able to say good-bye.

How much heavier and even more desperate you would feel if you believed everything is over after death. There is such finality attached to the thought that you can never see someone again, ever. Knowing we will see and feel one another again brings so much comfort. In fact, souls who have passed often come back for a final good-bye from the other side.

A girlfriend of mine called me after she had lost her adult son in a car accident. "Why, why?" was her desperate question. "He had his whole life ahead of him."

I meditated after I talked with her and saw him before my inner eye. I asked him if it were possible for him to see his mother again. He told me she should lie down in the bathtub and he would come back to connect with her. I thanked him and called my girlfriend. It took a couple of days before she found the strength to take the bath. Afterward she called me. She told me she had laid down in the bathtub and closed her eyes. A couple of minutes later she saw him. His eyes were closed and he appeared in different bodies. My girlfriend opened her eyes in surprise, then closed them again. She could still see the image of her son.

"What does it mean that his eyes were closed?" she wanted to know.

"I think it means he is calm and at peace. Perhaps he showed himself in different faces and clothes because he wanted to share with you that he has had many lives behind him, and he has more lives ahead of him. I think he tried to calm you and give you peace with that insight."

Unfortunately the calmness didn't last long. She spoke with many people about her son and her experience in the bathtub. Most of them didn't believe her and said it was just her imagination. They told her she probably created that image herself as a result of her pain. "You're having these hallucinations because of the pills you're taking. It was just your imagination. You just dreamed you saw him."

Eventually she concluded it was just her imagination. Great anger at God arose in her. The death of her son felt so unjust. Why did he have to die so young? The pain and shock at his unexpected end was overwhelming. It had come out of the blue and she'd had no chance to prepare for it.

What is more difficult: a slow dying process with prolonged suffering, or a quick death with no time to say goodbye? I asked my friend Jacqueline Snyder, "Is death easier or harder depending on whether you die quickly or it is prolonged?"

She responded, "I think it's important to know that people who die in accidents leave their body before the impact. The soul leaves the body immediately. I remember very vividly a plane crash in Seattle, where I live. The plane

crashed over a housing area and many people were desperate. I volunteered at an organization called God's Way To Life, where I met a wonderful older woman named Adelle Tining, who had the gift to contact souls. Many relatives of the people who had died in the crash came to her hoping to better understand what had happened to their family members and how they were doing on the other side. All the souls who came through reported they hadn't felt anything from the impact. They said they were immediately surrounded by a bright light and heard beautiful music. Some spoke to their angels who were nearby. The relatives asked all sorts of questions through the medium to make sure the souls to whom they were speaking were truly the people they'd known. Each of them felt uplifted and felt a sense of completion afterward."

My girlfriend Mon, an art historian, shared a similar experience with me. "When my mother was shot, she only smiled. She was without any pain whatsoever."

I was shocked when I heard this because I had no idea her mother had died so violently. She told me the whole story. "Every year in the fall, my parents went to Corsica. My mother's brother and his wife also went with them. One year in particular, when I was twenty years old, newly married and eight months pregnant, their travel preparations didn't come together easily. That year, my father didn't want to go to Corsica, but my mother was almost obsessed with going. They argued about it, but she couldn't be persuaded not to go. Even the trip was difficult. There were delays and problems with the car, which had never happened in any of the prior six years they'd taken this trip. My father was very upset.

"The evening my mother died, they went out for dinner. My mother's brother, my uncle, had cleaned his gun earlier in the evening because he wanted to go hunting the next day. The evening was joyful and they drank a lot of alcohol. No one really knows anymore exactly how much they drank. My parents and my uncle and aunt came home from the restaurant about midnight. They opened another bottle of wine at the house and were just having fun. My uncle and my mother always had kind of a wild relationship. They loved to play practical jokes on each other. My mother was forty-seven years old then, but they were still like young teenagers together. They were making jokes and laughing. She only did that with my uncle, never with anyone else.

"My mom had to go the bathroom. She stood up from the table and went to the bathroom door. For some reason, my uncle thought, 'I'm going to scare her.' He saw his gun lying on the floor. He picked it up and snuck up on her. He wanted to scare her with the click of the gun being cocked."

"But wasn't the gun loaded? Did he forget that?"

"Very good question. Somehow he must have forgotten. He pulled the trigger believing he just wanted to scare her with the clicking sound. As he fired, he realized the gun was loaded. But he thought he was shooting next to her head. That was not true. The bullet hit her head and she died.

"Many years later I talked with my uncle about that terrible night because I wanted to know if she was in pain and how she reacted. As he heard the noise of the gun fire, my uncle said he saw my mother laughing. At first he thought nothing had happened. He thought she was laughing because there was a large hole in the wall behind her. He explained to me that she leaned on the wall and laughed and laughed and laughed. All of a sudden her knees couldn't support her and she slid down the wall, still laughing. As she reached the floor her laughing stopped. She was dead.

There had been no pain whatsoever. She went from laughing to dying, which was very typical of how my mother lived."

"Have you ever felt her presence since she died?" I asked, knowing that in most cases this happens.

She nodded. "Yes. The funny thing was that, on the night of her death, I was spending the evening at my parent's house outside of Munich. For some reason, I wanted to be there."

"Why?"

"I can't explain it. I have no idea. That night I drove with my husband from Munich out to this little town to spend the night at my parent's house. Don't ask me why. In the middle of the night the phone rang. It was 1:30 a.m. and my Grandpa, who also lives in Germany, was on the phone. He told me my uncle had shot my aunt."

"Your aunt?"

"Yes. He was very upset. I tried to calm him down and told him I would call Corsica. So I called Corsica and a woman's voice answered the phone. I said, 'Mama?' When the woman said in a terribly sad tone, 'No,' I knew my mother had died. The woman on the phone was my aunt. Then I broke down.

"My husband was concerned about me because I was pregnant. It was a sad time for me. Twelve hours later, on Sunday at noon, I was still at my parent's house. I just couldn't bring myself to leave, so I lay down to take a nap. Suddenly I woke up because I felt someone touch my forehead. I opened my eyes. I realized I could smell my mother! Smell her! There was a special smell on her skin from her perfume. I couldn't see anything, but I knew and felt and smelled her. I said, 'Mama.' I was wide awake and it was completely clear to me that she was in the room with me.

That was her smell! The whole thing lasted for about ten seconds, but it felt so good to me.

"Something strange also happened with Mom's cat. Her cat reacted very oddly after her death. A week later, I brought the cat to the vet and he noticed she had a large kidney tumor. She'd been to the vet for a check-up just three weeks before and she had been completely healthy then. The vet couldn't believe it. On the day my mother was buried, about a week after she died, her cat also died. Isn't that interesting?"

"Her cat wanted to go, too."

"Yes, it sounds like that, doesn't it? You know what else was strange? My aunt told me that, on the day Mom was shot, they'd been lying on the beach in the afternoon. Mom said to her, 'You know, I really hate getting older. Wouldn't it be wonderful if I could die now? My daughter is happily married and pregnant. Everything is done.' You know Sabrina, my Mom was tired when she went to Corsica. Somehow she had finished with her life."

"You know Mon, I believe she knew her time had come. This urgent wish to go to Corsica, the conversation with your aunt—everything looks as though she was ready to move on, to leave the physical plane.'"

"Yes, I think you're right. The last year of her life she always looked exhausted. I do believe she was ready to leave."

It is our own pain, our own loneliness, that stays with us when someone we love dies. But it is also our choice to understand that our beloved one is more than just a body that has stopped functioning. He or she is a soul, an energy that never stops. Nothing that exists in the physical realm can disappear into nothing. That doesn't mean we should stop or shorten our grieving time and pretend nothing has happened. If it hurts, it hurts. But we can also ask ourselves, "Why does it hurt?" Sometimes it is our own fear of death. Or we may be in shock because things have changed so quickly and our fragile sense of security has broken down.

When one of our loved ones dies, questions about the meaning of life automatically arise. To stay in our pain and anger stops us from learning. Life is change—even if it is hard on us. To know that death is just a passing from one reality to the next, from one body to the next, often brings comfort. I always look at life as a long adventures trip. Somewhere in the future I want to go home. Some people travel for a long time, others for a shorter period. Some go home early because they feel homesick. Some of us travel in a group and some of us prefer to travel alone. Even if our travelling companions miss us, we know we will meet at home again. If you have not yet said 'good-bye' to the person that moved on, here is a way to do so: Hold a piece of jewelry the person once owned. Use a prayer to ask for a contact to say good bye. It always works.

152

Chapter Eleven

When tiny Angels are looking for a job and how big Angels can help tell a good story

It was a very special day. I had to get ready to go to Julia's preschool. Once a week, one of the children was allowed to pick their favorite book to be read by their Mom or Dad, and this time it was Julia's turn. Her favorite story was one I told her after her friend Mattie had spent the night with us. Mattie, an active six-year-old had made me her angel expert.

One busy Friday evening, Mattie was sleeping over and it was time for the children to go to bed. After the usual good-night story and our prayer, I left the room hoping both girls would finally stop whispering and wiggling and fall asleep. Was I wrong! For the next two hours I heard laughter, movement, feet on the floor and the light switch going on and off every half hour. I went to Julia's room and asked the girls to please stay in bed and be quiet. Of course, both of them were having so much fun they didn't want to fall asleep. They decided they wanted to eat ice cream at midnight. Because they were so excited about this, they couldn't fall asleep at all.

It was almost 11 p.m. when Julia came into the living room and said, "Mama, Mattie is crying so loud, I can't sleep."

"Mattie is crying?" I asked in surprise. "What happened?"

"I think she wants to go home to her Mama," Julia said,

sitting comfortably in my lap, happy her Mama was right there.

I carried my daughter back to her bed. We found little Mattie shivering and sniffling under her blanket. "Mattie?" I said quietly, as I stroked her blond hair. "Are you sad?"

"I want my Mommy," she said in a quivering but determined voice.

Oh no, I thought. Mattie's parents lived about a half hour away and the idea of taking her home in the middle of the night was not inviting.

"Please!" She pushed her blanket down so I could see her shaking, lower lip. "I want to go home to my Mommy."

I sent a prayer up to my angels: "Please, I need a really good idea to help Mattie calm down so she can fall asleep." I took a deep breath and suddenly I heard myself say, "Do you know the tiniest, littlest angel?"

"No-o-o." The answer came out slowly, but definitely curious.

"What do you think of this idea? I'm going to tell you a story about the littlest angel and if, after you hear the story, you still want to go home, I'll take you." And I prayed silently, "My dear angels, please let your story be very good because I don't want to drive Mattie home in the middle of the night."

Mattie thought about my idea and then agreed. "Okay. But afterward you promise you'll bring me back to my Mommy?"

"Yes, I promise if you want to go home after the story, I'll gladly take you."

Mattie lay on the top bed of Julia's bunk bed and I made myself comfortable on the floor so both of them could see me. "So," I said, beginning my story without the slightest idea how to continue, "there was this tiniest, littlest angel. She was so little the other angels who were invisible couldn't find her most of the time. That's how little she was. She was as little as the tip of a snowflake," I continued. "That's how little she was. She was as little as the tiniest grain of a sugar cube and the tiniest piece of cinnamon. The littlest angel even smelled a bit like cinnamon. But the littlest angel was very, very sad. She was bored. She had nothing to do."

Both girls stared at me curiously. Mattie stopped sobbing. In my mind, I thanked my angels. The story was going well. I was curious how it would continue.

"Each angel watches over someone. It's either a girl or a boy, a mom or a dad, an uncle or an aunt, a grandma or a grandpa," I heard myself say. "Some angels watch over dogs and cats and horses. Other angels watch over dolphins and hamsters. But the littlest angel had no one to watch over." I hesitated and I knew exactly why: my mind was interfering with the story. I decided to, once again, trust my angels. Nothing against my own mind—it's a wonderful instrument, but it is limited. My intellect is like a computer that only has the programs I have put into it. My mind has extraordinary logic, but my intuition, feelings, trust and creativity don't come from my intellect and should not be replaced by it.

"Go ahead Mama," Julia encouraged me.

I took a deep breath, and with it I welcomed the trust to say what came into my mind. Again, I let myself float and listen to the thoughts that came as I told the story. "It was a full moon, and every full moon all the angels met on a mountain top. Mother Moon looked like a huge cheese pizza and all the angels gathered together and danced and laughed and told each other stories they'd heard from people they know—

exactly as we tell our friends stories from the people we know and the things we've done."

From the top bunk came a very concerned voice: "But at the full moon, wasn't there a guardian angel around?"

"Angels can be in more than one place at the same time." I soothed her. "It's the same when you sleep. Your body lies in bed and you sleep while your soul goes into dreamland and has wonderful adventures. Sometimes when we wake up, we don't remember them, but they still happen. In the same way, one aspect of the angel is watching over you, while another aspect is hanging out with the other angel friends dancing in the soft moon light."

Both girls were satisfied with this answer.

"All angels look different. We humans are different, too. Some angels have huge rainbow wings. Some wear glittery white dresses. Some are covered with flowers. Some angels you can see through, while others are warm and fuzzy. Some laugh and dance, while others move silently. This night, the angels were sitting around in a circle telling their stories. In the middle of the circle was someone who was very, very sad. That must have been our littlest angel. She was so little, that—"

"—the other angels couldn't see her." Julia finished my sentence.

"Exactly." They didn't seem to be very sleepy yet, I noticed. "Why was the littlest angels so sad?" I asked the children.

"Maybe she wanted to go to her Mommy?" suggested Mattie.

"No, that's not the reason she was sad. She was sad because she had no one whom she could watch over. So, as the littlest angel sat in the circle with all the rest of the an-

gels, she asked, 'Why am I so small? It's not my fault that people are so big. I want to watch over someone, too. It's not fair.'

"Now, you should have seen the other angels. They felt so sorry for the littlest angel. They could imagine how she must be feeling. 'Well,' they said, 'how about if you come with us as our little helper?'

"'I don't want to be a little helper,' answered the littlest angel. 'I want to be a big helper!' The littlest angel twirled around in a circle, and rainbow colors sparkled from her. The other angels felt how angry she was. And then she flew away.

"The other angels were still speaking to the middle of the circle where the littlest angel had been. They didn't even notice that the littlest angel had left already. That's how little the angel was. Mother Moon looked down and saw her flying in long, sad waves through the air. The tops of her wings were flapping down and Mother Moon felt how sad she was. To give the littlest angel support, Mother Moon sent one of her very special rays. The littlest angel felt a tiny bit better, but she still needed help. Angels receive help exactly the same way people do: from God."

Mattie and Julia made themselves very comfortable in the bed.

"The moon ray stopped before a beautiful cherry tree with pink blossoms. They smelled very sweet and felt very soft. The littlest angel rested herself on a little twig. She cuddled up in the cherry blossom and used her wings as a blanket. She closed her tiny, tiny eyes. She took a deeeeeeeep breath and thought of God.

"'Dear God,' she prayed in her mind, 'How can I find someone whom I can take care of?' Then she became very quiet in her head. Very, very quiet.

"And God sent her a thought: 'You have a very special job, my wonderful, special angel.'

"'But what is my very special job?' asked the littlest angel.

"'You will find it when you search for it,' she heard in her little head. She felt God's love and it made her very happy.

"'If you say I'll find someone then I know I will.' In her mind the littlest angel gave God a huge kiss. Then she opened her eyes again. 'I gotta go,' she yelled at her friend the moon ray. 'I have to find my job!'

"Night time was almost over and Mother Moon called back her moon ray. When the moon moves slowly to the other side of the earth, of course she always takes all her moon rays with her.

"'Thank you, Mother Moon! Thank you, moon ray! See you tonight.' The littlest angel waved her wings happily at Mother Moon."

"Then the sun must be coming soon?" mumbled Julia.

"Exactly," I replied. "The littlest angel stretched out her wings and shot up like a spiral in the air, like a beautiful arrow. 'Hello, wonderful day. I'm coming!' She was singing and flying away. And there was Father Sun smiling at her.

"First the littlest angel flew to the East, where everything begins. She found a huge ocean. She saw the fish and the dolphins. She watched for a sign of her new job. But she only noticed that everyone was far too big for her. So after awhile she flew to the South, where everything continues. There she found a huge forest with lions and deer. Again she watched for a sign of her new job. But she only noticed that everyone was far too big. Then she flew to the West, where everything ends and changes. She found a desert and saw camels and elephants and watched for a sign of her new job. But she only noticed that everyone was far too big!

"So went to the North, where everything rests for a new beginning. She flew on top of a mountain and saw an eagle and a bear and watched for a sign that would remind her of her new job. But she only noticed that everyone was far too big."

"The poor tiniest angel," whispered Mattie. Or was it Julia?

"Hm, yes, she was very, very sad. Her wings got a little tired. Now it was time for Father Sun to leave that part of the world and for Mother Moon to return from the other side. The littlest angel flew back to the cherry tree where her moon ray was waiting for her. She rested at the foot of the cherry tree. 'What did I do wrong?' she cried, sadly shaking her pale, tired wings. 'God told me I would find my job,' she told the moon ray. 'But why haven't I found it yet?'

"Again the littlest angel tried to calm her thoughts so she could hear what God had to say. She took two deep breaths this time. Again it was very quiet. Then she heard a noise. Someone was crying! But where? The littlest angel looked around. Behind the cherry tree was a beautiful little house with a shiny red door, many square windows and an old fence around it. One window was open so Brother Wind could carry the sound of the crying child to the littlest angel. She flapped her wings very fast and, with the next blow of Brother Wind, she glided in through the window.

"A little girl lay curled up in bed, crying and crying and crying. The ears of the littlest angel were ringing—that's how loud this little girl was crying. Over the little girl's bed was her big guardian angel, who was trying to calm her down. But the little girl didn't seem to notice this big angel.

"'What happened? Why is she crying? And why aren't you helping her?' asked the littlest angel to the big guardian angel.

"The guardian angel shook her wings. 'I've tried,' she answered. 'She's afraid to sleep alone in her room in the dark, but I've told her she's never alone, that I'm always with her. But she's only focusing on her sad thoughts and she cries so loudly she can't hear me.'

"'That's really dumb,' said the littlest angel. She had heard a lot from children and knew what they would say in such a situation. The littlest angel flew closer to the girl and stared at her. 'Hm,' said the angel. 'Hm.' In her mind she was searching for an idea.

"Then she heard God say, 'Look at the girl. There's something only you can do. Look closely.'

"The littlest angel grew quite excited. 'What? What is it?' She stared at the little girl, who kept crying and crying and crying. Tears rained down from her eyes and her nose and the littlest angel thought, 'If she would just stop crying and start listening.'

"Then she noticed the little girl's ears and she had an idea! She turned around quickly to the large angel and said, 'I can help her. Only I can help her because I'm so little.' She flew directly into the girl's left ear. In her ear were many curves and circles and the littlest angel flew very carefully not to bump against something. At the end of this long ear tunnel was a little step. It looked like a bench. The littlest angel sat down and started to talk: 'Can you hear me? It's me. I'm your angel!'

"The little girl was just about to take a deep breath and continue crying. But in the middle of her deep breath, she stopped and thought, 'Is someone talking to me?'

"Angels, of course, can hear thoughts as if they were words. So the littlest angel answered, 'Don't be afraid, little girl. You're never alone. Your angel is with you.'

"The little girl thought she was dreaming. She sat up in bed and opened her eyes. No one was in her room. She looked around—now she was really scared! She wanted to start crying again so she closed her eyes because, as you know, you can cry much better with closed eyes.

"But the littlest angel kept talking. 'Hello little girl. I'm your angel.'

"'No, I wasn't dreaming,' thought the little girl. 'I can hear my angel in my head.'

"'We're always with you,' said the littlest angel. 'You just have to stop crying for a little while and listen to me.'

"And so the little girl stopped crying for awhile and tried to be very still.

"'Very good.' The littlest angel was proud of the little girl. She began to explain: 'In your world when something happens—something new or something old—you can always hear two voices in your head. One is afraid and, if you listen to that voice, you'll get more and more afraid. You'll feel lonely and said. And that's not very helpful. The other voice if full of love and hope. When you listen to it, you'll feel safe and happy, comfortable and full of hope. Now you can make a choice: would you like to listen to the voice that makes you sad, or would you like to listen to the voice that brings you joy?'

"The little girl knew exactly what she wanted. 'I want to listen to the voice that brings me joy. But,' she asked, 'how do I get rid of the voice that brings me fear? That voice is very, very loud.'

"'Exactly the way you change a show on television you don't like or that scares you. You switch the channels,' replied the littlest angel. 'It works in your mind when you think of something wonderful.'

"As the little girl listened to the little angel, she realized that listening to the other voice was what made her fearful.

"'It's very easy,' said the littlest angel. 'Each time you are afraid, just think of us and how much we love you.'

"The little girl made herself comfortable in her bed and said to her angel, 'But I don't know how much you love me.'

"The littlest angel replied, 'Just ask and we'll send you our love.'

"The little girl became very still in bed and asked the angel to send her love. All of a sudden she felt warm and comfortable. She felt great—just as you feel when you open a present and get what you really want. Or when you have a big ice cream cone on a hot day. Or when your parents do something really funny and you have tears in your eyes because you're laughing so hard. Or when a little kitten comes and touches you on your leg. Or when someone who loves you carries you around all day. That's how good love from an angel feels! So when you're sad, don't forget to think about the wonderful things you have in your life.

"The littlest angel explained, 'Your big guardian angel is always with you. Just ask to feel her and you will.'

"'That's wonderful,' thought the little girl. 'That's much more fun than listening to the terrible voice that makes me sad and fearful.' Now the little girl trusted her angel was always with her. Even if she were alone in her room, she knew her angel was there, so she was never alone. She was ready to fall asleep so her body could stay in bed while her soul went to dreamland to play with her friends and angels. As the moon ray shone into the open window, the little girl fell deeply asleep.

"The littlest angel flew out of the little girl's ear and stopped in front of the guardian angel.

"'You're wonderful,' said the guardian angel.

"The littlest angel was very, very happy. She was shaking and all the rainbows were coming out of her wings. The sound her wings made was like beautiful bells that sang proudly. 'I found the perfect job for me. I'm going to take care of all the children who are sad at night and tell them about their guardian angel, who always watches over them. That's my special, special job,' the littlest angel said happily. She hugged the big angel very tight. Well, as tight as a little angel can. But, you know, it doesn't matter how big you are or how big your body is, it's your mind and determination and love that are important. And our littlest angel knew that for sure." I heard deep sighs from both Julia and Mattie. "Good night my little angels," I whispered after I gave them each a kiss.

"And also to you my heavenly angels," I thought. I went into my office because I know I had to write this story down.

I printed twenty copies of this story on my favorite sky colored paper and took them with me to Julia's preschool. This was the story Julia wanted me to share with her friends. With the copies, each child could take the story home.

Julia's preschool class was a combination of all different cultures and religious backgrounds. The wonderful thing about angels is that they are recognized by each culture and

religion. Whether Muslim or Jew, Christian or Buddhist, the heavenly messengers are cherished and treasured by every one.

I opened the door to Julia's classroom and Julia jumped up and ran toward me. "Mama, Mama! They have a chair for you and the teacher said I can sit in your lap."

I greeted the three teachers and all the kids who were sitting around me in a circle on the round carpet. In Julia's school it was customary for parents to take an active role. Just recently, when they were looking for a new preschool director, I was one of four parents asked to be present while the director of the school conducted the interviews. The parents also asked several questions. Mine was, "Do you believe trees can talk?" It was enlightening to watch the reactions of the people applying for the job. Two laughed nervously as they glanced in my direction. It was clear they thought I was a little weird. One refused to answer the question, saying she didn't believe children would really ask such a question. The last one looked at me and responded without blinking an eye: "I would like to know from the children how trees talk to them."

"I like her," I said to myself.

In Julia's school a lot of attention was paid to the students' individuality, understanding different life-styles and types of people and how to communicate.

I asked the children if they had ever felt angels before.

"Yes," said Mattie. "When I was sleeping over at your house." She was grinning ear-to-ear as she looked proudly at her friends.

"Would you like to feel your guardian angel?" I asked the class.

"Yes! Yes!" Everyone was excited.

"Good. Then I need you to lie down and close your eyes."

Julia wanted to sit on my lap, so we could both look at all her friends. It is hard to describe how beautiful it is to see a whole class of children lie down to meditate. Anyone who has ever worked with children or has children knows how tough it is to have a group of five- and six-year-olds lie down, close their eyes, not move and be quiet. I was very touched and thankful to see this. One glance at the surprised teachers Linda, Francis and Michele showed me their own amazement.

"So-o." My voice was soft and gentle. "Now take a deep breath in. Very deep, right into your belly button. Then take your breath and throw it out again." I knew I didn't have much time. Fifteen children wouldn't lie down with their eyes closed for very long.

"Now imagine above you is a huge, huge rainbow. You stand underneath it and see the wonderful colors around you." Julia was sitting motionless on my lap and even the teachers had their eyes closed.

"Now ask your guardian angel to send you a feeling. Then watch how this feels in your body." I had never tried this with a group of children before and was very curious about their reaction. Adults usually had a feeling of peace, love or calmness. I was curious what children would say. Some of them were deep in concentration, some smiling and others had their mouths slightly open.

Sam opened his eyes and said, "Wow, that was fun! There was a little tickling in my belly. It was funny. Are angels funny, too?"

"Yes," I acknowledged.

"They want us to have fun." Rachel who was lying next to Sam, smiled and said, "I felt a tickle in my nose."

I smiled at her.

"I felt someone was playing with my hair. That was sweet."

"I felt very warm, like when someone turns on a heater."

"Someone tickled my ear."

"My angel gave me a kiss."

The children were all excited. As they tossed out their different experiences, their smiles and the glow in their eyes showed me how much fun it was to feel their guardian angels.

David had a question that was dear to his heart: "If I do something bad, what happens to my angels? Will they still like me?" Deep concern marked his face because he was a little rascal and quite mischievous.

"Angels always love you. It doesn't matter what you've done."

David had a big grin on his face.

"But," I continued, and David immediately looked concerned again. "Angels also want to help you to be the best child you can be. That's why you should listen inside to your guardian angel before you do something."

David nodded with understanding.

"Are angels real?" asked Erica. "Can we see them?"

That was a good question. "Yes," I responded. "Many people can see angels and most of them feel them. Others can hear them. It doesn't make a difference if you feel them, hear them or see them. They're still always there."

And here we go with my favorite theme...

"My friend says angels don't exist," Noah said in a quiet voice, and all eyes turned toward me.

As the angel expert, I wanted to have a good answer. "Help me," I asked in my thoughts to my angels. I waited for a second until a thought was sent by my angels. "Look, Noah, you can't see angels most of the time because they are like air. You don't see air either, but air is still there."

He nodded with understanding.

"Or love. If you love someone you also can't see the love, but you can feel it. Isn't that true?"

Everyone was satisfied with this answer. And I was, too.

"Well, are you ready for your angel story yet?" The kids came closer and I asked Julia to give copies to her friends to take home.

Ten minutes later, one of the first mothers knocked on the door. She was right on time since we had just finished the story of the littlest angel.

"Mommy, Mommy, I felt my guardian angel!" Miranda jumped up and ran to the door to hug her mother.

"That's great," she answered. Then, without seeing me, she asked, "Was Sabrina here?"

168

Chapter Twelve

How rainbows help us connect with Angels and about children who talk to Angels

That evening Julia and I were sitting in the swing in our back yard. I told Julia I was writing a new book.

"What are you writing about?" she asked.

"I'm writing about angels," I replied. "Could you ask your guardian angel to help me a little?"

She pulled her cozy blue blanket a little closer to her chin and said, "But, Mama, I don't know the name of my angel. Why don't you do the rainbow thing so I can find her."

I would usually begin by suggesting people imagine they were in a meadow. I asked them to notice the plants, the smells, the trees. Then I asked them to look up and see a rainbow. This rainbow sent down its colors into the body, which brought healing. What happened after that was different each time. Sometimes I had them imagine they were at a river, sometimes a mountain, or under a tree. Then, the angel would come down from the top of the rainbow. In all my guided meditations, I trust my angels to send me an inspiration.

Julia is often around, when I conduct meditation classes or when I help people by giving guidance about the process of dying. In the beginning I always wanted Julia to leave the room because I wasn't sure how these talks would affect her. I had never heard anything about death when I was a child. If someone was dying, I only heard that so-and-so was sick and then later they disappeared. There was a short period of crying and that was that. When we met relatives of the deceased, it was always a little bit uncomfortable. There was hardly ever any talk about the person who had died as soon as the funeral was over. The relatives just looked at each other with a certain glance that seemed to say: "We know." As a child, I often thought, "This dying thing is weird. Something terrible must happen because no one speaks about it."

Julia, of course, never left the room for long when I talked to people about dying. She would leave for a short while because I had sent her out of the room. But then she would come quietly back and listen to whatever parts of my conversation she could hear. I wasn't sure whether it was good or bad for her to be confronted with death at such an early age. What could she understand and what not? Would she have nightmares about it? I always asked her after each conversation if she had any questions. But she always said, "No."

I think dying and the process of passing was very natural for Julia—much more natural than it was for me as a child. She had no nightmares and no fear of talking about death. She also had no fear about dying animals. She participated with compassion and interest when we buried a dead bird or mouse. We said a prayer and she knew the body was empty, like the shell left from a caterpillar that had become a butterfly.

One day her friend Sam was visiting and I caught the children killing spiders. "What are you guys doing?" I asked.

"Sam started it," Julia answered quickly.

"But they're just spiders," said Sam.

"I don't care who started it, Julia. It was your choice to do it, too. I want you to think about your decisions before you do something." I looked from Julia to Sam. "How would you guys feel if someone huge came from above and mushed you?"

"I wouldn't like that," Sam said softly.

"But, Mama," Julia protested. "The spider just gets a new life."

I couldn't believe it! Was this the result of teaching her about reincarnation—that each person and animal has many lives; that we never die, but go from one body to another, spending the time in between with God and our angels to rethink our old life and prepare for the next? Oh God, how should I answer this one? I looked at the face of my daughter, whose smile said, "See Mama, I learned a lot."

Finally an answer entered my mind. "That's right Julia. But the decision when to leave this life and choose another should be made by the spider—not by you." Thank you, God. I loved this answer.

"Okay, Mama," she replied. Sam, too, promised to think about this.

As Julia and I sat on the swing, she said, "Come on, Mama, I want to go to the rainbow, too." She closed her eyes and made herself cozy under her blue blanket.

I said a prayer aloud for both of us. "Dear God, dear angel, please let me be one with your wisdom and your love that is always there so free for us to receive. May my words help Julia to connect with her guardian angel. Amen.

"Okay, my darling, now take a deep breath in ... and a deep breath out ... deep breath in ... deep breath out ... and then imagine you are in a beautiful meadow. You see the flowers and some butterflies, some birds and ... look at the colors of the flowers ... and keep your eyes closed. What colors do the flowers have?"

"The flowers are blue and pink and green and yellow," replied Julia.

Each of my meditations is different. I always trust my inspiration and my guidance. I let my thoughts run freely and repeat whatever comes into my mind without analyzing it. In my prayer I had declared to God my goal, my wish, for this meditation. Naturally God listens to me. This I learned from Samantha, my friend who speaks with animals and who heard as a child that God was her father—and, of course, our father listens if we ask him for a favor. So, asking God to help me guide the meditation for my daughter allowed me to trust that whatever thoughts came to me would guide Julia to what she needed. And in this meditation she needed to go to the top of a mountain. "At the end of the meadow you see a mountain," I said. "Can you see it?"

Julia nodded.

"At the bottom of the mountain is a door. Open the door and tell me what you see."

She was quiet for a little while, then answered with a smile, "I see a lot of animals, like in a jungle."

I was glad she had no fear of these animals. "In the middle of this mountain are some stairs that go up. I want you to go up them. There you'll find a wonderful, fantastic, beautiful castle. Tell me when you're there."

"I'm there, Mama."

I knew it was not important for me to understand every aspect of this meditation: What do the animals mean? The castle? The stairs? If I thought about it too long, I would analyze the meditation, and I didn't have to do that. I trusted my angels knew what they were doing. "In this castle is a room with a rainbow." This thought came into my mind so

I shared it with Julia. "Look for this room and go inside ... Are you inside?"

"Yes."

"There is a bell. Whenever you ring this little bell, your angel will come to you."

I watched Julia carefully. Under her eyelids, her eyes were moving rapidly, an indication she was in her altered state. "Is your angel there?" I asked gently.

"Yes."

"Ask her what her name is."

"Jennifer."

"Ask her to hug you and tell me how that feels."

Julia was quiet, then said, "It feels like when Papa and you hug me."

"Now you can ask her a question."

Julia was quiet for a moment. She opened her eyes.

"What did you ask her?" I wanted to know.

Julia was cuddling closer into my arms. "Where she lives."

"And what did she answer?"

"In a cloud house."

"Did you see it?"

She answered enthusiastically. "Yes, Mama. It was shiny and sparkling and it was see-through. Just like a cloud, but with much more sparkle."

"What did your angel look like?"

"She also sparkled and was very shiny. She had long, long hair."

It was getting cold in the garden and almost time for bed. "What do you think, Julia: would you like to take an angel from my altar so you will always be reminded of Jennifer?"

She nodded with excitement. We walked to my meditation room. Julia spent ten minutes in front of my altar checking out each angel. None of them seemed to satisfy her. All of a sudden I noticed a little angel's bell I had forgotten about. "Look, look! There is a bell with an angel on top of it. Just like the bell you found in your meditation when you asked for your angel. Would you like to have it?"

I was hoping for an enthusiastic response because I found this bell fascinating. But, no, Julia chose a picture frame with angels around it. "I want this, Mama, because then I can draw the angel myself!"

We went to her room so I could watch her draw her angel. Now it was really time to go to bed. Julia put the frame with her angel on her side table. After brushing her teeth and putting on her nightgown, she asked, "Mama, can I please have a lesson in mastery?"

Almost every night after we prayed, I gave her a lesson in "mastery," as I called it. A master is in control of all her movements, and Julia was learning to control her body and not follow each impulse. It lasted as long as she could manage not to move, sometimes five, sometimes twenty minutes. It didn't matter if her body was itching or scratchy or ticklish.

I was given this idea in one of my meditations. Next to love and joy and comfort, I wanted to share with my daughter the importance of discipline, concentration, and focus.

When I traveled I taped a lesson in mastery for her to listen to each day I was away. It started with relaxation techniques: "Feel your little finger ... your ring finger ... your middle finger ... and so on." It also included some chakra exercises: "Above you is a beautiful, shiny sun ... the light of the sun comes through the top of your head into your body ... and goes down your back, through your seat to the front."

Julia loved this ritual. Once she explained to one of her

girlfriends: "If you want, my Mama will also give you a lesson in mastery, but you can't behave like a baby."

The next day, my friend Sunny came to visit, with her adult daughter April and her five-month-old son Zachary. Sunny was a hypnotherapist. April and Zachary lived with Sunny and her husband Stan. Zachary was a dream baby. He laughed a lot and slept even more.

Sunny, April and I sat at the kitchen table cutting apples for a fruit salad. "We brought you an angel experience for your book," Sunny said.

April asked, "Have you ever heard of children who talk to their invisible friends?"

Here it was again! I had just been thinking about this and now she had brought up the subject. "Yes," I said. "But I have not met anyone yet who can talk to me about them." Julia had never mentioned any invisible friends. When I asked her about it, she said she didn't have any.

"Today is your lucky day."

"Did you have an invisible friend?" I asked April.

"Yes. You get a double version of this story—one from Mom and one from me."

"Who wants to start?"

April nodded at her mother. "Why don't you start? I'll interject if I want to add something."

April tasted one of the grapes while Sunny started her story. "April was a very quiet child. She was a dreamer. She loved to spend time with herself. She spoke to her dolls and stuffed animals. I think you were about three years old when we were driving in the car and you mentioned Tuman."

"Tuman?" I asked.

"Yes," April replied. "Her name was Tuman. I can't re-

member clearly when I met her for the first time. It seemed she was always there and I always had someone to whom I could talk. You know, I was an only child."

"Did you know Tuman was invisible to others?" I wanted to know.

April looked up. "You know, in the beginning I thought everyone could see Tuman. Later I noticed that wasn't so. I don't remember exactly when I understood, but I realized she had the choice if she wanted to be seen by me. And I knew that other people couldn't see Tuman."

"What did Tuman look like?"

"Tuman looked a bit like me. We were always the same age. When I was three years old, she was three. When I was six, she was six. She was a little taller than me and she had my light blond hair—hers was a little longer but it had waves like mine."

"And her face?"

"You know, I don't have a clear recollection of it. I can't tell you much about her face." April shook her head.

Sunny smiled at April. "We had a chair at the table for Tuman. She always sat with April in the back seat of the car. Once we were in the checkout line at the grocery store when, all of a sudden, April turned around and said, 'Hi, Tuman!'"

"Was Tuman around a lot?"

"Almost every day. Tuman appeared suddenly in different places. One day when I brought April to preschool, her teacher said she wanted to talk with me. She explained that April was not paying attention, that she never knew when she was asked what the teacher had been talking about. She was a day dreamer and the teacher had no idea what to do with her. When April came home from preschool that day, I asked her why she wasn't paying attention in school." Sunny turned to April and asked, "Do you know what you said to me?"

"Yes. I told you Tuman went with me to preschool and we played together most of the time. I remember you explained that I had to talk to Tuman and tell her she couldn't come to school with me anymore, that this was my time to learn. But she could come anytime after school."

"Did Tuman honor April's request?" I asked.

Both nodded.

"Mom, do you remember the story about that guy in Mexico?" April turned to her mother.

"What about Mexico?" I was curious.

"Back then, I was an assistant to a private detective. We were searching for a man who had stolen a lot of money and then disappeared. Somehow I had the idea to ask Tuman. So that night I asked April if she could ask Tuman where this man was."

April was nodding. "Tuman showed me a picture in my head. I described what I saw. I also heard words like "Mexico" and "Oaxaca." I described a certain house I could see in my mind."

"What's Oaxaca?"

"It's a little village in Mexico that really exists," Sunny explained. "April described the house Tuman showed her, and we found the house. It turned out the man we were looking for actually spent time there."

"Did you find the man, too?" I asked.

"No, we were too late." April interjected, "You know, I specifically remember how concerned I was about the information I received from Tuman. I was about seven years old and I was afraid it was just my imagination. I'd never heard of a place like that before and it was my mother's boss who needed the information. I wasn't quite sure that everything Tuman told me was the truth. But one week later Mom told me they'd located the house and the person had actually been there. After that, I was completely sure whenever Tuman told me something that it was the truth. All my doubts were gone. I knew I could always trust Tuman."

"April, is there a special experience you remember the most?"

"You mean besides Mexico? Oh, yes—when Mom asked me if she could also see Tuman."

I turned to Sunny. "Could you?"

"You know, that was very exciting. I was, of course, curious about Tuman and April said, 'Okay, Mom, you can see her.' So we went into her room and I closed the curtains so the light would not be so bright."

"Why was that?"

"I knew how to see auras and I knew it was easier when the light was not so bright. So I asked April to call Tuman. We sat down for about three minutes, very quietly. Then all of a sudden I saw an orange light. Sabrina, do you remember the Enterprise on Star Trek with Captain Kirk? When they beamed the people in and out of their transporter room?"

"Of course! That was one of my favorite shows on television when I was a child."

"Do you remember when they beamed the people into the transporter room, there was always a little flash first, and then after a few seconds the body completely dematerialized? That's how it was with this orange light. It had the height of a child and it was down to the floor. This orange body, which was flickering, moved from the end of the bed to April's closet. I told April I saw an orange light flickering by her bed and moving to the closet. April told me this was Tuman."

"Sabrina, that was another indication that Tuman really existed, because now my mother could see her as well."

"Did anyone besides the two of you ever see Tuman?"

They looked at each other and pondered the question. "Yes," Sunny said after a moment. "There was my friend Anita. April and I lived in her house after I separated from my first husband, April's father. When I was away on a business trip in San Diego, about two hours from where we lived, I heard on the radio that a fire was burning in a forest close to our house. I was terribly concerned because the police had blocked all the roads and I couldn't drive home.

"Finally I got my friend Anita on the phone. She told me everything was all right and April was sleeping. She hesitated. After a short while she said, 'You know, something strange happened. April was sleeping very restlessly in my bed. She was tossing and turning when, all of a sudden, a little girl appeared out of nowhere at the end of the bed. She was blond and had braids. She walked over to April's side and gently touched her back. Immediately April stopped tossing and turning and slept peacefully.'"

"'Oh, that's Tuman,' we told her."

"I'd love to see her, too," I told my friends. "Sunny, did you ever doubt that Tuman really existed?"

"No." Sunny shook her had. "I had a very sound spiritual base. I knew there were angels and I knew there were entities we couldn't see with our eyes, but that could communicate with our children. I didn't believe other parents when they said it was just a figment of the imagination."

"Is Tuman still with you?" I asked April.

"When I meditate, she often comes."

"Is she still as old as you?"

"She has changed. In the beginning she was a girl. I must have been around twelve years old when I noticed she had become female and male at the same time. She almost disappeared during my puberty. Now I feel her once in awhile when I'm alone and I concentrate on her. But she's not as present as she used to be."

"And how old are you?"

"I'm twenty-three. Last year, actually, she helped me avoid a head-on collision with another car."

"What happened?"

"I was driving through the city on my way home from work and I came to an intersection. The traffic light turned green and I heard Tuman's voice in my head: 'Slow.' So I eased up on the gas pedal and even stepped on the brake a little. There were no cars as far as I could see so I was surprised to hear Tuman. Just as I entered the intersection, all of a sudden, a car sped through it, red light and all. If I hadn't slowed down before I reached the intersection, he would have slammed into me."

"What do you think Tuman is: an angel or a spiritual guide?" I asked both of them.

"I don't know if there's a difference. Angels may be able to take one form or the other, depending on what is more convenient," Sunny answered.

April added, "You know, the most wonderful thing about Tuman is that I always have the feeling someone is there. I'm never alone. That has really influenced my life. I don't have periods of loneliness, as some of my friends have. Even if I'm alone, I'm not lonely. This other world is also my world."

As if right on command, Zachary walked in from his nap … in this world.

After they left, I thought about my childhood. Did I have an invisible friend? No, there was no one. But I did have a wild imagination that I shared with my friends. For example, I imagined I had a horse in my cellar. But these things were all from this world.

The only thing I clearly remember that always came into my mind when I was a child was the feeling that my life would be easier when I was an adult. "When you're an adult, you'll laugh about it." I heard that sentence over and over as I went through my little and big childhood crises. It became my mantra and I reminded myself to repeat it over and over: "When you're an adult, you'll laugh about it."

I imagined myself being an adult and having high heels and a dog. A poodle. This seemed to be the epitome of an adult woman. High heels and a dog. I don't even want to analyze that one!

I once had the feeling I had visited myself as an adult while I was a child. That comforted me. Time, as we know it, is a logical following from seconds to hours to days to weeks to years. However, that is only our perception. Time and space can be changed. Isn't it true that an hour can seem either short or long depending on what we do? If we wait for someone, an hour takes forever. If we're having fun, the hour goes by fast.

We can also imagine that time as we know it will be changing. Three years ago I studied hypnotherapy. When you study it, you go through the experience of being hypnotized daily so you can understand what clients may experience. During one of these sessions, I saw myself as an adult woman vis-

iting myself in a dream when I was a child. I was twelve years old and I was lying in bed, restless. I, as a thirty-eight-year-old woman, sat next to the bed and touched my twelve-year-old cheek. "Everything is going to be all right," I heard my adult self say to my younger self. "When you are grown up, it'll be easier. You'll see." I had the odd feeling that I was, at that point, my own angel.

As I came out of the hypnosis to my adult consciousness, I spoke with my teacher Stephanie Jordon about it. She had often heard about cases like this. "It seems to be that the adult 'I' speaks to the child 'I' as a means of comfort. Psychology believes that you only take care of your child self in your mind. If you understand that time and space can be altered, however, there is another possibility—that you can actually move through time and space to comfort yourself."

I found this explanation fascinating and felt at ease with the idea that I could comfort myself.

Chapter Thirteen

About an Angel who is a Master and about how my eyes suddenly see through a body

My husband and I were sitting in front of the living room fireplace. My eyes followed the flames in the fire. "Fire romances the soul," my friend Jacqueline once said to me. As I looked into the fire, I thought about the enlightened master Zarathustra.

He was the one who taught me that I create my own life; that I'm not the victim of circumstances; that my thoughts, words and actions form my life. He taught me how important it is to have clear and beautiful thoughts. He tought me the universal law of cause and effect; that everything I do will, one day, come back to me. As I think of him, I feel movement deep in my body, like waves that move from my stomach to my heart.

Zarathustra.

About two thousand years before Jesus Christ was born, the prophet Zarathustra lived in human form in Persia. He always taught outside with the sky and the universe above him; with fire, the symbol of life, in front of him and with the earth, the mother of our body, beneath him. He was the first to speak about a soul. He was the one who declared how important the control of thoughts is in your life. "Good thoughts, good words, good deeds," that's how simply he described life. The three wise men who greeted the new-born Jesus were Zoroastrian priests, which is what scholars now proclaim. Zarathustra and Zoroaster are two names for the same person.

When Zarathustra was a young man, legend tells us, he went swimming one day. He came out of the water and lay down on the shore to rest. He fell asleep and saw a huge angel. This angel gently led him on a trip. During this journey, he saw all realities—not only the human one, but all the realities of the angels and different dimensions. He saw the universe and all the other universes. He was shown things he had never dreamed of before. When he woke up, he remembered each part of the journey. Through realization of how the world and our lives function, he became enlightened.

When I was a child, my Uncle Alwin called me "Zarathustra, my woman." I accepted that as something my uncle said, but I never thought about it. At least not until my massage therapist Malcolm mentioned the name Zarathustra twenty-five years later. His friend Jacqueline Snyder allowed Zarathustra to come through her body to speak to us. I immediately got goose bumps as Malcolm talked about Zarathustra. How amazing that our bodies remember before our consciousness does! My goose bumps , as a sign of adrenaline which is sent out by the body not only out of fear, but also out of excitement, reminded me of a long-ago promise.

I have met many facilitators, more commonly known as "channels," people who allow souls from other realities to speak through their bodies. In each case, the medium moves into a trance state and someone without a human body uses the body of the medium. Sometimes only the voice is used; at other times the whole body is used. Of course, it is only with the agreement of that human being. How well the in-

formation from the other side comes through depends on the integrity of the person as well as the level of mastery achieved by the one speaking from the unseen. Imagine a space ship coming from another planet and landing on earth. The inhabitants of this space ship meet a dog, a little child and a wise forty-year-old woman. They ask each the same question: "How do you live on earth?"

The dog would probably say, "Well, there's lots of food here. I eat twice a day. Most of the time I sleep. I have a black cat whom I love to chase. It's great fun. And I love to chew on things. My fur itches a lot because there are little animals in it."

The little child would probably answer, "I always have to go to bed early. I can't eat sweets anymore. My Mom dresses me every morning and Daddy makes breakfast. Then I play in my sandbox. I love my little stuffed animal, Hershey. When Grandma and Grandpa come, they bring me a coloring book."

The wise forty-year-old woman would probably say, "We are here on earth to learn to express God in human form and to make this world into a paradise."

Let's further assume that the beings in this spaceship only meet the dog. What would they think about us? For this reason, it is important who channels whom. Only enlightened masters who inhabit a human body for a short period of time can give enlightened answers to our questions. They don't judge or scare us, nor do they tell us precisely what is going to happen. If we choose to grow as we have grown so far, an enlightened master can see our potential, but he also sees the choices we have. We choose our life and make daily decisions that change our future. Therefore, how our future looks depends on the choices we make now. An enlightened master also knows there are no good or bad decisions. Whether we are able to make the best decision depends on how much we have learned. That is our freedom—and our future.

Zarathustra is such a master. These masters are souls like us, only a little quicker in their realization that we are all part of God. Well, okay, a lot quicker! Jesus, Buddha, Moses, Zarathustra, Mohammed and many, many more. Each of these souls has reached enlightenment.

Once I asked Zarathustra, "How is it that you're so advanced and have realized yourself, while I'm still here?"

Zarathustra looked through Jacqueline's eyes at me and said very gently, "That's what *I'd* like to know."

I had to laugh. Yes, why did I need so much time?

Ten years ago Jacqueline was reminded in a profound vision of a sacred promise, like a covenant, she had made before her birth to share her body with Zarathustra. She had the choice to keep this promise or not. Since she was married and had two sons—one a teenager, the other just seven years old—it was a decision that concerned her family as well as herself. She decided to keep her promise and accept all the consequences. It took a great love of God, discipline, focus and the understanding she would spend her life in service.

For weeks, she was taught by spirit to trust in just one prayer and in her love and faith in God—regardless of what was happening around her. Slowly, just as one learns to play a musical instrument, it became possible for Zarathustra to use Jacqueline's body. First it was only her eyes, later it was her voice, still later her upper body and finally he could even walk with Jacqueline's body.

Jacqueline Snyder is not someone who would lease out her body as one would rent out a guest room. She is an author, respected visionary, spiritual leader, teacher, public speaker and lecturer. She spoke at the Earth Summit in Brazil and has organized sacred events and conferences. She was asked to be the spiritual advisor of the Cherokee in Georgia. She respectfully carries a sacred pipe and travels to the holy places in this world. She is far too active to give her body to just anyone.

Jacqueline is a living example of what Zarathustra teaches. She reflects Zarathustra's teachings in everything she does. She shows what is possible when you live with love, compassion, and discipline—the model of a sacred life. Because of this, she has been a great inspiration for me.

Zarathustra also kept his sacred promise: to speak to us through her. In the beginning, I was a little nervous about meeting him. Some people had told me they did not believe in channels. They thought these people just imagine someone else is talking through them.

I had never actually met such a person, but I was confident my intellect and senses would clearly tell me the truth. I didn't think anyone could be fooled for a long period of time because an enlightened master would, of course, have better answers than someone who was just pretending. He knows more, loves more and explains more.

When I was in Zarathustra's field, I felt him. There was a movement in my stomach. Deep inside of me, a wave found its ways through my cells. There was a strong desire in my heart and, at the same time, an easiness I had never felt before. Emotions sometimes burst forth, like a volcanic eruption. Often times, a sentence Zarathustra spoke touched me so deeply I cried. Deep inside, my soul remembered the truth, long before I understood it.

The first time I was with Zarathustra, I just watched him

carefully. I analyzed each of his words and movements and asked him questions (such as "What happened with my girl-friend, Olga?") without giving him any information. He would explain the situation in great detail, and his advice was wise and caring. I listened to him for hours when he spoke at vision quests and workshops and answered other peoples' questions. His wisdom was endless. Each question was answered to the satisfaction of the questioner. He could explain complicated theories within such fields as medicine or physics with so much clarity that an expert became stunned. One scientist had a question I didn't even understand. This scientist's mouth dropped open as Zarathustra responded to his problem.

In the beginning, I would get very tired when I was near him. I couldn't explain this to myself. Now I know that my sensory field needed to get used to his high frequency. After a few weeks, I became more used to him and able to detect how the frequency in the room changed. When he came into Jacqueline's body, I felt first some tickling in my body, similar to what I feel when I go into a hot bathtub. All my cells were suddenly active and ready to receive input. Now that my sensory field has been trained, I can feel him even when I have my eyes closed. I am able to get more signals when I concentrate on him. Because I have also raised my own frequency, learned to control my thoughts and contact the love I feel for my fellow humans, I no longer get tired.

I notice that I get a little restless when I write about Zarathustra. I have the feeling I want to protect him. I want to watch out for the opinions of others who don't know him. I hear his voice in my head as I write these words, "Don't be concerned. I understand doubt and question. God is cursed daily. We are in good company."

Yes, that is true. How often he understood my own doubts! Once someone asked him, "Why should I listen to you? How do I know you tell the truth?"

He smiled and replied, "I don't tell you to listen to me. You have the choice to stay or go. Make your choices with not just your mind and intuition but also ask your soul to be part of it. Trust the depths of your soul."

That woman decided to stay. At the end of two hours, she had tears in her eyes and so did I.

I learned a lot from Zarathustra and Jacqueline. The most important lesson was to control my thoughts.

"Each person," Zarathustra said, "has the possibility for every wish to be fulfilled instantly. But what would happen if each of your wishes were fulfilled?"

I immediately thought of the hundreds of drivers who would disappear from the face of the earth.

"You need to learn to control your thoughts. Each negative thought brings you further from the fulfillment of your wishes. Think about whether each negative thought is worth it. Come back to the childlike enthusiasm that will reenergize your life. This energy creates miracles."

Once I complained about a friend who didn't listen when I gave him a piece of my advice. I wanted to shake him until he listened to me. Wasn't there a way I could make him listen to me so he would do what I told him, because I knew what his problem was?

Zarathustra's answer, which is so often a question, was: "Did he ask you for advice?"

I got uncomfortable. "Well, not directly. But it is really important for him to listen to me." I noticed I was even more restless because I knew exactly what Zarathustra wanted to tell me with his question.

"Did he ask?" he repeated.

Finally I shook my head. "No."

"You can only give advice if someone has the space to receive it."

I understood. It was like a closet. You cannot put more clothes in than what fits. If you do, everything will fall out the next time you open it. "But does that mean I shouldn't say anything anymore?" I asked, confused.

Zarathustra replied, "Say to him: 'I have some ideas about your situation. Would you like to hear them?' With that, you give him a choice."

That was smart. It made sense. If I had thought of that earlier, it would have saved me a lot of frustration.

Zarathustra taught me that I didn't have to follow my feelings such as anger, fear or loneliness each time they came up. Each feeling we've ever had is stored in our cells. We can exchange any feeling we don't want for a feeling we want. We can prepare ourselves by choosing three feelings that bring us love and joy, and then concentrate on these feelings when we want to get rid of the others. Never forget that one of the greatest gifts for humanity is the possibility of choice. We have that choice!

I thought about the feelings I like. My love for Zarathustra and Jesus. My love for my husband and daughter. My love for my family and all my sisters. It worked. Each time I got angry, felt lonely or bathed in self-pity, I thought about my love for God and my family. Immediately a feeling of relaxation came over me, as after a massage. Each of these feelings was different. My love for God was a little different from my love for my husband or my child, my family or my sisters. I had a choice! This is something I'm never, ever going to forget.

Zarathustra taught me it's not my job to find out what is wrong with other people, what their problems are or what they still have to learn. "Always look for the potential in the men and women and children you meet as you cross paths. Never search for their problems or bad habits."

He also said, "Never say, 'I don't know that.' Always say, 'I would like to know that' or 'I'm curious how that works.'"

And he said, "Whenever something happens in your life, wait and say, 'I find only blessings in my life. What blessing does this situation bring me?' Expect only blessings in your life."

When Zarathustra lived in Persia two thousand years ago, only men were allowed to learn his wisdom. Women had different responsibilities. But Zarathustra acknowledged the same right for all souls, regardless of whether they had chosen a female or male form. He always taught under the open sky and spoke loud and clear, knowing that many women were hidden nearby, listening in secret to his teachings.

One day he went to these women and promised them he would come back and teach them. When Zarathustra told me this story, I listened to him as you would listen to a fascinating fairy-tale. Then he leaned forward and looked into my eyes and said, "And you are one of these women."

In that moment, I instantly found myself in Persia. I smelled eucalyptus and the scent of flowers. I experienced the heat and felt loose linen on my skin. A deep feeling of homesickness brought tears to my eyes. Longing struck me like lightening in a storm.

Oh, yes! I remembered—all of a sudden, without warning, just like that.

Afterwards I was exhausted and confused. My longing,

my missing God, the feeling that I was here on earth by accident—all these were a hundred-fold stronger. Again I felt the melancholy feeling that had never completely left me, even in the happiest hours of my life. Sad questions arose: "What do I do here? Why am I here? There must be more than this, and I want to find it!"

The thought came into my mind: "If you are looking for it, you will find it." I felt as though I were on a scavenger hunt, "Here is a piece and there is a piece." Wouldn't it be great if I could jump over some years and have the result already in my hands? The result! Deep satisfaction, deep peace, childlike joy and understanding for everything. Why was this so difficult? Why did it go so slowly? Shouldn't I know more by now? "Stop it!" I told myself. I had chosen negative thoughts, therefore I had *made* it difficult. Each negative thought pulled me away from my soul. As soon as I decided to let go of the negative thought, another feeling came up—a feeling of gratitude and great awe.

There was so much more than I had ever thought possible, so much more than I ever imagined. My life was now more exciting and caring than ever before. Was that how the Universe worked? Had that two-thousand-year-old promise been kept? Was that why my uncle had felt inspired to call me throughout my whole childhood, "Zarathustra, my woman"? So that, when I was thirty-three years old and had met my massage therapist Malcolm, I would remember when he talked to me a year later about his friend, Jacqueline Snyder and about Zarathustra? Were these the long-term plans my soul had made with God? Good-bye, coincidence! I knew I could never believe in coincidence again. If the Universe works in this way—our angels take care of us and God loves us—it seemed to me that all we need to do is have trust that our search and desire will bring us fulfillment.

My thoughts from the past slowly brought me to the present. My eyes were still fixed on the fire burning in the fireplace. I had lost myself in the power of its light. To see. Yes, finally to see all angels, all feelings, all fairies, all little people, all thoughts. I was so curious and impatient.

Malcolm had made an appointment for me to see Zarathustra. As I sat in front of him for the first time, there he was in Jacqueline's body—in a white silk top and pants, with her long black curls pulled back into a pony tail. His legs were crossed in a yoga position. He asked me to come to him and hug him.

I knelt in front of his chair and leaned slowly toward him. "Can this all be true?" That thought entered my mind.

Zarathustra opened his arms to embrace me. Held my head in his hands and looked deep into my eyes. "Yes, Yes, Yes."

He smiled at me and I said to myself, "I hope he is not reading my thoughts."

"Yes, Yes, Yes," he said again. I could see the twinkle in his eyes.

I cannot clearly remember what I asked him at our first meeting. I forgot in all the excitement to turn on my tape recorder. I just remember I spoke of my deep wish to see more.

"You will see more than you ever dreamed." That sentence is the one I remember most.

"When?" I asked.

"Within a year you will see more and understand more. You will find that your desire and your astonishment about life and the world will fulfill your wishes."

Yes, he was right. Didn't I learn within a year to see auras?

I took another log and placed it on the fire, after respectfully asking the fire's permission. I looked deep into the flames again. I knew Jacqueline could read the fire and wondered when I would learn that, too.

I had to laugh about myself. Yes, there it was: my never-ending curiosity. Or was it just the memory that there was so much more and that each wish would help me awaken these insights?

I made myself comfortable on the couch and leaned on my husband, who was focused on his book. I thought about an experience I'd had about nine months after Zarathustra came back into my life.

I had just finished my study as a hypnotherapist and was practicing on my girlfriends. One of them was Kim, who lived in Washington, D.C. and was visiting me for the weekend. Kim was a beautiful woman in her mid-thirties. We had met on our first vision quest, a three-day retreat on a Colorado mountain top spent in silence, prayer and teachings. When I met Zarathustra for the first time, he spoke to me about a weekend that Jacqueline was organizing for twenty people to find their vision. It was a traditional Native American ritual in which young men in puberty were sent alone into the wilderness. They had no food or clothes with them and spent the time alone. These quests sometimes took a week. At the end, the young men entered into manhood. Performing this ancient ritual in the sacred silence of nature, these young men found the direction of their lives. When Zarathustra spoke about this mountain, I knew I wanted to go. I just had to convince my husband.

My husband was concerned I would turn into a weirdo. Maybe I would shave my head, wear only orange and follow some false guru. My household altar he could live with.

At least there was a picture of Jesus on it. But it was too much for him to accept that I would go with a group of strangers for a long weekend on the top of a mountain, without a phone and no way to reach me.

"What do you want up there?"

"To find myself," I answered with agitation. I was often irritated when I was asked why I did these kinds of things. I felt I was being personally attacked.

"Can't you find yourself here, in our backyard?" He was slightly annoyed.

I felt like a little girl who had to ask her dad for permission. I was getting angrier with each passing second. I tried hard to sound calm and offer my understanding, "You see, it's like when you go with your friends to play tennis."

"I don't go away for a weekend without you to play tennis," he responded dryly.

That was true. What should I say now? "Well, why don't you come with me?" I suggested.

"I don't have time for that!" he barked back.

For weeks, the mood between us was strained whenever I talked about the mountain. I only knew: "I have to go. I have to go. I have to go."

Finally I'd had it. I lost it. After the hundredth discussion about this mountain, I looked angrily at my husband and screamed at him—I who never screams: "And if it's the last thing I do, I *am* going to this mountain. Whether you like it or not!"

So now it was out. I took a deep breath to prepare for his storm. "Okay, then I won't make plans to travel this week so I can be here with Julia."

I couldn't believe my ears. Couldn't we have come to this understanding a couple of months earlier?

My husband and my daughter brought me to the airport.

My sleeping bag was under my arm; warm underwear and a couple of throw-away contact lenses in my luggage. I had bio-degradable soap and a new notebook. I flew to Denver, rented a car and drove two hours to Steamboat.

We met at the house of some people who were also going on the vision quest. I was one of the last to arrive. Half of us were over forty and not at all weird. I must admit, I was expecting a little more weird. One person in the group even introduced himself as a Catholic priest. If Richard had only known that!

And then there was Kim. She had long, blond hair, my height and my eyes and many other characteristics similar to mine. We sat together in a corner and started to talk. It seemed we had known each other for a very long time. More people came and we needed more chairs. We both jumped up at the same time to help. Something needed to be brought to the mountain. We both raised our arms to show we had space in our cars. On the top of the mountain we were asked to find a tent we felt drawn to. Kim asked me if I would like to share a tent with her and her friend Teresa. Kim and I immediately had the same feeling for each other—the feeling of a long-lost sister.

I asked her what had brought her to the mountain.

"My angel sent me. He said I would find family here."

I had goose bumps when she said that. A month later, we were still in close contact. Kim visited me in Los Angeles. She worked as a nurse, but she was also an incredibly talented painter.

"Why do I hesitate to show my paintings?" she wanted to know.

With my new skills as a hypnotherapist, the answer was clear: "Let me find out."

Hypnosis is like detective work. It is exciting and deeply

satisfying. You always find the "perpetrator." Somewhere in our past, experiences are buried that contributed to who we have become. All our fears have a source. It is our choice to find this source, which can be deep down in our childhood or in a former life. The most fantastic thing is that we ourselves know the source. Sometimes we have difficulty connecting with this source when we are awake and active. Through hypnosis we can open the locked door to our unconscious so the search can begin. Being hypnotized feels similar to the moment before you fall asleep. Even though almost all my clients remember what they have experienced, I tape the sessions for them to take home.

All his life, Sigmund Freud believed hypnotherapy was useless. Shortly before his death, however, he acknowledged it as one of the most important forms of therapy. A good hypnotherapist gently guides his clients through their unconscious with understanding and love. The therapist never follows his own ideas. For this reason, I always say a prayer with my client before we start, asking for God's help and guidance to work for my client's highest good.

Kim made herself comfortable on the couch in our guest house. Back then I didn't have a large studio. She closed her eyes during the prayer and I followed her breath as I led her into therapy.

Breathing in: "With each breath …."
Breathing out: "you imagine …."
Breathing in: "how clear air …."
Breathing out: "comes into your body …."
Breathing in: "your lungs are filled …."
Breathing out: "and you …."
Breathing in: "relax …."
Breathing out: "deeply relax …."

My voice was soft and slow as I followed Kim's breath. When I talked to her, I watched her eyes behind her closed lids.

Breathing in: "and through your feet …."

Breathing out: "all your worries and concerns …."

Breathing in: "are moved out through your breath …."

Her eyelids moved faster, a sign of the altered state in hypnosis. I heard the tape moving as I recorded the session. I leaned forward a little more to watch her breath. I spoke to her almost automatically, which often happened after I offered my prayers, whether for a guided meditation or a therapy session. I trusted my intuition. Even if my mind occasionally swallowed hard, so to speak, when I heard what I said, I knew it wouldn't connect with my client's soul because its understanding of what my client needed in that moment was too limited. Through my prayer, it was my soul that connected with the other soul to help them and honor them.

Of course, my angels—still unseen by me, but nevertheless felt—were in the room. Their presence felt like a little tickle on my skin, which could easily be overlooked if I weren't quiet. And there was a feeling in my heart as if time stood still. Then there were high frequency sounds, like the ones I'd heard when I was younger after I'd spent a long time in a discotheque with loud music. Afterward I would hear funny waves in my head for a long time. I always wondered what these sounds were. Did everyone hear them, but just didn't talk about them? Hm. When I felt my angels I always had to take a deep breath. It was an automatic wish to fill up my lungs with this peacefulness.

Kim lay relaxed on the couch. There was a small wrinkle on her forehead, at her third eye. Her hair was in a braid and her hands were slightly open along side her body.

Breath in: "You find yourself …."
Breath out: "under a rainbow …."
Breath in: "and you let the colors …."
Breath out: "slowly enter your body …."

She had reached the phase where I could go deeper into her unconscious. "Next to the rainbow you will find a being … a guardian angel … Nod if you see it …."

I saw her nod.

"Describe how your guardian angel looks …."

Kim's voice sounded soft and sleepy. Sometimes she swallowed the syllables slowly. "It is more male than female … large … smiling … stretched-out arms … purple dress …."

"Your guardian angel will touch your hands and give you a feeling. Describe that feeling."

She was quiet for a long time, her face highly concentrated. She enjoyed the time. "Peace … family …." Tears of joy ran down her cheeks. She took a deep breath in. "My heart is very soft ... unbelievably soft …."

"Your guardian angel will now guide you ... all questions, all situations will be explained by your guardian angel …." I let her walk on a time line so she could go back in her past to the point where her problems had started. "Where did the fear in your paintings come from?"

From a life as a painter, she told me. She had been a man and she had been ridiculed because of her paintings. "They were too far advanced for that time period," she whispered. "People didn't understand them …."

"What happened to you?"

"They killed me."

I looked tenderly at her face and knew what this understanding meant. It was the understanding that this fear still lingered in her. During my studies, I had been hypnotized many times and I always learned from the lessons each life had brought me. There was deep remembrance, like the one Kim had just had about the life in which she was an artist who was killed because he showed his paintings.

Knowing about this situation would loosen Kim's fear because she now had an explanation in her consciousness. The wrinkle between her eyebrows was gone. Then, all of a sudden, I noticed her eyebrows were gone as well! I couldn't even think, I just watched how her body changed in front of my open eyes. First her eyebrows got darker and thicker. Then her hair did the same. It was still long, but it became black and curly. Her body was see-through, like milky glass. I could see the couch underneath it and I could see triangles, circles and spirals of different colors and intensities in her body. I tried desperately not to blink. I was afraid it would just last a moment and I didn't want to miss anything. I wanted to see as much as possible. Her head was changing again. This time she was a woman with reddish hair. The only thing that didn't change was her mouth when she spoke: "I see myself as a woman ... I am in a garden ... I am sad ... My child is sick ...."

My eyes started to burn. I couldn't hold it any more: I had to blink. I opened my eyes as fast as I could. I still couldn't believe what I was seeing. I was blessed to see Kim still had her see-through body. Her lips were the same, but the rest of her body changed every time she spoke.

"Look for a tree and sit under the tree and watch the situation from above .... You are only a visitor in this life ... Nod when you are under the tree," I told her.

The red hair nodded. "Why is your child sick?"

"No food."

"Why?"

"My husband is a painter … No one wants his paintings … We are hungry."

"Viewing it from a distance, what did you learn from this life? Ask your angel, he will help you."

After a long pause, I saw the triangles move in her body and a long light wave went from her throat down to her navel.

"He said that I learned in this life ... that I could ask for help and it would be given …."

"Did you ask for help in that life?" I asked gently.

"No … my pride …."

She had learned to ask for help. This is probably also why she had asked for a hypnotherapy session. No life is ever wasted. I continued to watch Kim's body with excitement for almost half an hour. Her body changed in front of my eyes and became Kim again as we ended the therapy session. Her body slowly became more dense and I could see the difference between the couch and her jeans. Her hair became her hair and her upper body closed like the cover of a treasure chest.

A second later, she opened her eyes. "Thank you."

"You thank me? I have to thank you!"

As I looked at the fire, I thought, "I should have drawn her body." But I had been much too excited to even think about it.

"You did not need to draw it," I heard in my head. "You will never forget it."

Yes, that was true. This experience was very important in my life. Until that moment, I had always had a little doubt that I might just be imagining all of it. Maybe my imagination went wild and maybe my wishes created what I experienced. But after I was blessed to see how Kim's body looked in a different dimension, in broad daylight for over thirty minutes, it was clear to me that this was a gift from God. Because I had seen it with my own eyes. If this were possible, it must also be possible to see my angels. Right?

I slowly let the fire burn out and followed my husband to our bedroom. Maybe tonight I would see my angels. Who knows …

Chapter Fourteen

About "normal" Angels, Guardian Angels and Master Angels and about how we are linked with Angels

I called Jacqueline Snyder's *Sacred Life Ministries* office. "Please, I need some time with Zarathustra. I have so many questions about my angel book."

Some months ago I had asked for an appointment with him, but nothing had happened. I knew why. Zarathustra only gave appointments if you had first done your work internally. The only time he had given me advice for my book had been seven months before.

Jacqueline came to San Diego from Seattle once a month to teach a spiritual class and to conduct a healing service. It was a diverse group of people who had heard of either Zarathustra or Jacqueline. Some of them had been with the group for many years. San Diego is a two hour drive south of Los Angeles. So, once a month, usually on a Saturday or Sunday, I left Los Angeles at 10:00 a.m. and arrived in San Diego by noon. Jacqueline taught the first part of the class for two hours, then Zarathustra taught for an hour and a half. When Zarathustra was finished with the teaching portion of his class, he made himself available for questions.

My angel question was at the tip of my tongue for the entire class period. I believed I had done all I possibly could regarding my desire to see my angels. I had prayed to see my angels. I believed in angels. I felt them. And I was able to see them in my inner eye. I had even written my wish

list—because I believed that everything my soul desired, everything I focused on, would happen to me. I wanted to show the Universe with my wish list that I was ready to concentrate on seeing my angels. Jacqueline had once said, "Write down for twenty-one days what you want. Each day, the same list. Without any 'if's' or 'maybe's.' Without any concern that this is not possible. Without thinking this is crazy. If you ask the heavenly powers for help, they are ready to assist you. Your belief gives your wishes the power to materialize. If you doubt, however, you pull back your wish with each doubt. Then nothing happens." At the end of the wish list, I had to write down, "I am ready to give up everything that doesn't support this goal."

I once spoke with Samantha about the power of thoughts and wishes. She said that every successful person had a vision or dream about how the end result would look. It was with the help of this dream or vision, and with the belief that it would happen, that all wishes were fulfilled.

I used to admire people who were able to do twenty-five things at the same time—to write a book and a screen play and a couple of poems, or host a talk show, a magazine show and a children's show. Or to follow one idea and have another idea on the side. I wanted to do that, too. But whenever I concentrated on several different things simultaneously, nothing happened. Each seemed to take away the other's power.

On my last vision quest, I spent two days alone on a mountain in Montana after the time I spent with my friends. The spirit world taught me about focus and concentration.

I flew to Pryor, Montana to spend some time on the land where my friend Tana Blackmore had Sacred

Ground. In the middle of this holy mountain was a group of teepees. During the warm months you could stay in these teepees. Many people would spend time around the fire with the Native Americans, talking about visions and pipes. They learned how to make a medicine bag, play the drums and pray to the Spirit of the Land. Some came, as I did, to seek their own vision on the mountain.

When Jacqueline organized another vision quest, I wanted to spend some days after the four-day quest alone on the mountain. I had my sleeping bag, my pipe bag and a small luggage bag with me at the L.A. airport. An hour before departure, I was waiting in line to pick up my ticket. The airline had sent it to me by mail, but I had never received it. I called and called and had a funny feeling the whole time. They kept telling me there would not be a problem and my ticket would be reissued. I had a magazine with me, so I did something I usually never do: I read while waiting in line.

Finally it was my turn to see the woman behind the ticket counter. I explained my situation to her and she told me the plane was fully booked. There were no seats at all.

I couldn't believe this was happening. I felt as if I was failing my spiritual path. I started to cry. How could I miss my plane when I wanted to go to the mountain to pray? How was that possible? I screamed in my head to my angels, "Do something! Do something! Help me!"

But there was no way. The ticket agent told me I was already too late. I told her I had been waiting for an hour, but that didn't make a difference. Some hours and some planes later, thank God, I finally got a flight out. I landed in Billings and Tana picked me up. She noticed my restlessness. I told her what had happened, but she was also unable to explain why.

Tana brought me to the mountain where my friends were already waiting, and I immediately bombarded Jacqueline with questions about why I had missed my plane. She looked at me intensely but didn't say anything. I could see she wanted me to think for myself first.

As we sat around the fire, I asked Zarathustra. The only answer he gave me was: "It is easier than you think."

After days of teaching, followed by long hours of silence, I still didn't have an answer to my question: "Why had I missed that plane?"

I was hoping that the time alone on the mountain would help me. Tana, my sister in-spirit Sharon, and my sister Susanne, who had come from Germany to join me on this vision quest, went up with me for the initial ceremony. We brought a couple of apples and two water bottles. We sat down to pray. I asked my angels to send me a sign about which direction I should go. In my inner eye, I saw a butterfly dancing. I knew this meant a butterfly would show me the way.

I opened my eyes and told Tana, Sharon and Susanne about my vision. They nodded. I looked around and about ten seconds later a butterfly appeared. I was very excited. How perfectly the Universe worked!

We followed the butterfly up the mountain. It seemed to wait for us each step of the way. Then, all of a sudden, I couldn't see it anymore. I waited and prayed, and it appeared again. After we had walked for about twenty minutes, we came to a beautiful open area with a large stone in the middle. The butterfly circled the stone four times and sat on top of it. I asked the butterfly, "If this is the place where I should spend my time on the mountain, please stay. And, if not, please fly away."

The butterfly stayed and I put my pipe bag down. Tana, Sharon and Susanne said good-bye. They promised to light a candle and pray for me.

I sat on the ground, thanked my butterfly and started to meditate. I listened for a while to the sound of my breath and then watched myself from above. I went higher and higher until I could see the whole mountain. I saw Montana from above, then the United States, then the world. I asked my angels, "Why did I miss my plane?"

"Focus must never be sloppy. Don't forget that!"

"Of course, I was reading a magazine! I wasn't concentrating on catching the plane. I was concentrating on reading." I suddenly understood.

"If you want to concentrate on something, your focus must be a hundred percent. Everything goes in that direction. Each thought, each word, each deed. This creates the power that makes everything possible. If you divide your focus, you divide your power and each second thought, each second word and each second deed becomes involved with your wish. Then it takes double the time to finish your project. The more projects you have, the less you can focus on them. Dance at one wedding. Focus on one goal and it will happen faster and quicker than you ever dreamed. "

After a couple of days, I left the mountain with one of the most important lessons of my life: focus must never be sloppy.

Shortly after, I had a chance to practice this lesson while we remodeled our house. At the same time, I was supposed to be focusing on my book. But that wasn't possible. I knew I had to focus a hundred percent on the renovation, other-

wise the house would never be finished in six weeks. Afterward I would focus on my book. But why was it that, when I focused a hundred percent on my angels, nothing happened? Why?

In class I stood to ask Zarathustra my question. Zarathustra looked at me and said with a smile, "I hear you and I've heard you for a very long time."

I smiled back. "Zarathustra, I believe everything I focus on will happen. I wrote my wish list for twenty-one days, and each day I wrote that I wanted to see my angels. Why can't I see them? What am I doing wrong?"

Zarathustra moved his hand toward his chin as if he were going to stroke his long beard from two thousand years ago. "Hm. Why do you think you did something wrong?"

This was one of his trick questions. He wanted me to realize something, but I didn't know what it was. "Maybe you have an idea?" I asked him.

"Oh yes, very certainly I have an idea. But first I want to know why you believe you did something wrong."

"Well, because I'm very good at manifesting. Because things happen when I focus on them and wish for them. And because I've learned not to believe others are doing something wrong, I assume instead I did something wrong, or I didn't understand something yet. Besides, time is running out. I want to write a book about angels and I haven't ever seen any."

Zarathustra smiled gently at the frustration in my voice. "There are many books about angel experiences. That's nothing new, is it?"

I knew he was leading me somewhere with this discussion, but what did he want? For this reason, I answered very slowly, "Yeesss …?"

"How do you think the readers will feel if they read about experiences others have had but that they've never had?"

"Well, they will probably be as surprised as I am. Why?"

Zarathustra lifted his head. "Ahhh."

"Ahhh? What Ahhh?" I said to myself. Some in the group were laughing. It was that kind of understanding laugh that occurs when the answer is so blatantly obvious you can't help but chuckle at the person's inability to see the answer. Zarathustra still smiled in my direction.

"They would wonder, like me. Why?" I repeated the last thought to myself.

Since I had missed this chance at enlightenment, Zarathustra helped me. "If you had seen your angels already, your book would only share those experiences, and not how to get there."

Slowly, slowly something opened up in my mind. Zarathustra continued, "You have to describe the way. Tell how you searched for your angels. Take your readers with you on this journey. Then you will not just be showing them the end result."

I had tears in my eyes. Of course! "Will I see my angels?"

Zarathustra leaned slightly forward and looked deep into my eyes. "Hmm. It'll be very exciting. Isn't that true?"

"Yes," I replied. I didn't ask any more questions because I knew he would not give me any more answers. It depended on me. It depended on my wish, my desire and what I was willing to do for it.

"We will talk about it later," he promised.

And that later was now. "My book has to be finished in three weeks and I still need more information," I faxed

Jacqueline. As if Zarathustra didn't know that already.

Obviously it was the right time. Jacqueline was coming to Los Angeles three days later, so she could spend the night at our house and the next morning Zarathustra would talk to me about angels. I prepared a chair for him. When Jacqueline schedules readings by Zarathustra, it is a very sacred time. She always wears a white silk tunic top and white silk pants in honor of Zarathustra's presence in her body. First she sits there herself. Then, after five minutes of prayer, she leaves her body. As she leaves, her upper body falls slightly forward and then is completely still. After about a minute, you hear a deep breath arising from low in the abdomen, as breath is brought back into her body by Zarathustra. Her eyes are closed and it is always beautiful to watch as Zarathustra slowly inhabits her body in a gentle, yet powerful way. First his head moves upward, and his hands move in a rhythmic, purposeful fashion. Finally his eyes open. It takes about a minute before he can bring the room into focus.

I sat on the floor in front of Zarathustra. Next to me was my tape recorder, which I had checked at least ten times to make sure it worked. A candle was nearby. Zarathustra looked tenderly down at me and said in a voice that was different in tone and accent than Jacqueline's, "Blessed be unto you child. You still sit with the wonderment you had in the temple. Do you know it is wonderment and curiosity that add to the great vortex by which the Masters can reside among you?"

I thought he was speaking about how I had met him during his lifetime as Zoroaster/Zarathustra in Persia. My heart was soft and a fleeting memory arose from deep inside. I didn't know how important wonderment and curiosity were.

But, if I thought about it, it was logical because they were the means of all evolution.

Zarathustra continued, "What do you know about the angel you want so much to see? Let's begin with that."

"I know the angel is there."

"You can change 'the angel' to 'he.'"

"He?" I asked. "So my guardian angel is male," I said to myself. Well, that was a beginning. Zarathustra was nodding. "I know he is here," I continued, "that he cares for me..." Suddenly I realized how little I knew. I was sad. "That's all I know."

I took a deep breath as I felt the tears building in my eyes. Zarathustra smiled gently. He understood my sadness. I took my time and felt the desire for more wisdom and more knowing move through my whole body. "Are angels male and female?" I asked finally.

"Indeed. You could say they are integrated; that is their vibration. They can express themselves as one or as the other. On a great soul level, this is true. But, generally, angels reside within one particular gender. The one you call Michael is, indeed, Michael, and the one you call Gabriel, is Gabriela. And they also hold that image for themselves."

"Do they have relationships between females and males, as we humans have?" I asked.

"No. They experience love in a different way. Their love is ethereal. It does not lead to physical bonding as human love does, because they do not need to reproduce as you do. But they connect through frequency; they have frequency compatibility."

Yes, I knew what he meant by that. We have an electro-magnetic body. When I am happy and in love, when I help others and enjoy success in life, I feel lighter. If I am sad, unhappy or lonely, I feel heavier. My vibration changes and expresses itself in a feeling of lightness or density. This also means I can change my vibration by doing things that make me happy, thinking positive thoughts and separating myself from things that do not support my higher vibration.

Zarathustra continued, "Let me explain this a little further. Their vibration is at the level of knowledge and compassion. It is the highest domain and it holds the image of humanity in a perfected divine stage, until that image is not only superimposed on humanity, but integrated and expressed. Given this understanding, you would have angels with different domains, would you not?"

I nodded. "I understand that angels hold a perfect image of us until we, souls in human form, can match that image and hold it. This is why they are helping us on several levels. Angels are a role model for us." I thought to myself, "What a role model!"

"Very good. You may proceed," Zarathustra encouraged me.

So much different information was coming together. What, for heaven's sake, should I ask next? I decided to ask: "When there are angels who have different domains, do they serve humanity as we do? Doesn't that also mean they are able to raise their vibration through good deeds and reach a higher frequency just as we humans do?"

"Much better. This is what you should be asking. Very good. To say that angels 'earn their wings' is a very sweet expression, but it is more accurate to say they earn vibratory frequencies. When you do good deeds, don't you feel better? And in your betterment, don't you feel happy? Don't you feel lighter? When you live and think from that lighter place, it becomes your new domain. But if you become angry, you simply fortify a deeper, more dense state. Correct?"

"Yes." I had felt that often. A wrong word from someone and—bang!—I was down. More recently, it didn't happen as much. I was more aware when a person wanted to "drag me down" and I didn't accept that anymore. I had more understanding for the other person, for their need. With this understanding, I didn't take it personally—something that would have been nearly impossible before.

Zarathustra continued, "You reach that higher realm through your deeds. They determine where you reside. It may be only a moment in the beginning, but in time it will last longer—until this domain becomes your new home."

"How does an angel start to build up his frequencies?"

"An angel starts with the love of God and a willingness to serve the physical realms with the love of God. Therefore, angels do not reside wholly in the unseen realms. Do they?"

I was confused. I admitted I didn't understand.

Zarathustra nodded. "When humans begin to act as I have just stated, they evoke an angelic vibration within themselves because they have risen to this level. They integrate the human and angelic realms."

"And then we see angels!" All of a sudden I understood.

"Then you can see them. Also, humans become more angelic. Listen and listen well. When humans become more angelic, you can see them or not see them. I will explain, but I wish you would have waited to ask this. Yes, I am saying that humans who have reached a level of service in the angelic realms can find themselves in more than one place—because they can be seen and not seen. It is not more difficult for them to be unseen than it is for angels to be seen."

Wait a minute. Did I understand that right? If we raised our vibration through service to humanity and through our love of our fellow humans, we would be able to be seen or not seen? And then we could be at several places at the same time? Zarathustra nodded at me. He was reading my thoughts again.

"Does an angel choose to be seen or not seen?"

"An angel chooses to be seen or not. How long an angel can be seen is determined by the vibration of the environment they have entered. This is why angels can stay longer with children than adults."

"Were angels humans before?"

"Angels are at different levels. Some have never been humans and never shall. They hold the divine image of God eternally in the form of the image of man. Understand?"

"Yes, I understand. Angels show us how we humans can be like angels but still hold the human physical form."

"Some angels have committed to be in the point of light of the highest vibration of God. This has been interpreted by humanity through various visions to mean they are to the right of God. Therefore, they give the human image to that divine essence. This is the ultimate place of vibration. You would call these archangels."

"Are the archangels in this position because of their deeds for humanity?"

"The archangels are part of the original expression of souls who were retained to hold an image to which man could aspire. Because of the evolution toward male dominance, they became male. If the world were female-dominant, they would have been female. It was not God's determination that they be male."

"Will they change their gender now that the world is getting more in balance?"

"Angels have no need to change their gender because male and female are only a matter of impression. It is not a matter of gender."

Of course, I understood. We saw them as male because everything powerful was male.

"Will there be greater balance in the future?"

"They have always been balanced. It is a matter again, don't forget, of your perception. The integration will take place over time through your perception. For that is what it is."

I had to laugh. Of course, how stupid of me. Why should the angels change? We need to change what we think of them. "How does an angel get created?" I asked.

Zarathustra again stroked his chin and his invisible beard and answered with an understanding smile. "An angel is the point of light that vibrates to the frequencies of various domains, according to the desire and intent. They fulfill many levels. Understand?"

"Yes, Zarathustra. But aren't humans also points of light?"

"Ah. That is what I said at the beginning. I will explain so you can understand more thoroughly. You are points of lights that vibrate to allow your thought perceptions to formulate growth matter—what you would call dense matter or physical matter."

"So, we can create our physical life, here." I thought.

Zarathustra continued: "Given this understanding, you hold to the potential of your point of light, as well as to the thoughts and deeds of the angelic realm. First you must evolve to the state that exists between the point of light and that which is dense—which is the angelic realm. That is what I said earlier. The more deeds and thoughts of great love you have, the more you elevate yourself in your heart.

Then you are closer to that vibration and to integrating your own angelic vibration. You begin to feel more and more kindred to it until you have fully awakened to it. As the whole world evolves closer to this point, you have more visualizations of your angel. We are now at a closer proximity than at any other time."

Okay, so that must mean that, when we reach our own angel potential, we come closer to our angel frequency.

Zarathustra nodded as he read my thought.

"I will give you a childlike visualization. If God were here," Zarathustra lifted his left hand and stretched it out, "—which of course he is not—and humanity were here," he lifted his other hand down, "then the angelic realm would be in the middle."

"Ah-ha. So the more we as humans behave like angels—which means to have understanding, to serve, to show love—the closer we come to this angelic vibration. Then communication between humans and angels will happen more often."

Zarathustra nodded and put both hands back into his lap.

"How do an angel and a human choose each other?"

"Again, when I speak of vibration and frequency, there are various degrees. Angels often evolve in and out of the lives of different individuals. When you change, the world evolves. But evolution takes place when the individuals are able to raise their frequency. Angels of different frequencies work with them. Angels who initially assist a person are later free to work with others."

"So is it correct that many angels and angelic beings have worked with me until this point?" I understood more as I asked the question.

"But of course," Zarathustra replied. "They vary according to different dynamics. One's guardian angel would not change throughout a person's life. The one who holds the vibration of your ideal will hold that place throughout the entirety of your lifetime and through all your incarnations. They hold your image at a high level of existence that allows you to move into the place of mastery. Other angels reveal greater mastery that overrides and governs the structural frequencies. This is in your awareness because now you are at a level where you need more information how to achieve mastery while still in human form and how to evolve into the Godhead. Therefore, your awareness of angels will give way more and more to the masters who reside within the place of illumination, and who have evolved from the human realm into that point of light. You will learn more about this from the Nazarene, the Enlightened One whom you call Jesus Christ."

"Does this means there are also "normal" angels who were never humans, who help us in our daily growth? And guardian angels who are always with us, holding our ideal of the perfect soul in human form? And master angels who have lived in human form, who show us we have the possibility to be such a master angel—like Jesus, Moses, Buddha, and yourself, for example?"

"Indeed," replied Zarathustra. "This is not to say that masters are higher than angels, for that would perpetuate a hierarchy and not allow a master to speak directly to humanity—which is not the case."

I could see that.

"In fact, you do not need to be elevated to the state of the divine because it is always within you and you can choose in every moment to dwell there. You can think from there and act from there, and become one with the great brotherhood about which I have spoken. Of course, that term also

includes what you would call a sisterhood. It is a realm of beings who have transcended human experience and, by keeping their focus on the divine, extend heaven into all physical, emotion and logical responses to God."

This also meant that Jesus was not only the son of God, but also one with God and with all the other enlightened masters. Together they formed the Godhead. The fantastic idea was that each of us has this Godly spark within us. We can all choose to go into this realm through our love and our active service for humanity.

Zarathustra explained further, "What you call paradise, or heaven, is not separate from you. Paradise is included in your bodily existence through your thoughts, words and deeds."

Chapter Fifteen

About Angels who visit our children's bedrooms and when we are ready to see Angels

I looked at the list of questions in front of me. I had only half an hour with Zarathustra. I decided to ask about the famous sparks of light children see. "When children see these little sparks in their room, are they parts of angels?"

"They *are* the angels. The point of light has the possibility to change into the form of an angel. The angel point of light can grow into a larger light and take a shape to interact with the child. But it all begins with a point of light."

"Should I tell a child to focus on the point of light and watch how it gets bigger?"

"It is better for the child to focus on the feeling of love they feel in their heart for God. Because the point of light comes from that. If they focus on the love, the point of light will respond to that. Their intention should always be to interact with all life from this point of view."

"Is this the same for adults?"

"It is the same for all people. It is most important that it be a feeling coming from the heart chakra. This way the point of light can only be an angel."

"How can people get in contact with their angels? Through that feeling in their hearts?"

"Yes, the feeling of their heart, which is love; and within

that love you can sent out the greatest invitation to an angel, don't you think?"

"I believe that, too." I said with a smile. "Is that what I should do in the guided meditations in my workshops?"

"That is one right way. And it can always continue to grow in various different ways. When people sing, the melodic tone that passes through their body raises their vibration to a higher frequency. Every organ begins to vibrate and shimmer with light. Sometimes when people hear a choir, they feel they are having an uplifting experience. Because they are in a higher, fully balanced state, they can more easily perceive angels. They may even weep when they feel God present in the chapel. People would say such a choir is wondrous."

He looked deep into my eyes. In his special way, he told me I should put more music into my workshops.

I nodded back. "I understand," I said in my thoughts.

Zarathustra leaned back quietly.

"Do angels evolve by doing good deeds?" I asked.

"Yes. You say they evolve, but it is better to say that the frequency domains elevate. This is also true for humanity. Your frequency domain elevates."

"What do angels do besides watch over us? Or don't they do anything besides that?"

"They exist within glory. In the domain of the angelic realm, do you know glory? Do you know promises and hope? These are thoughts that feed the domain of the angels. The angels continually thrive on the vibration of that domain, and then send it back to us. Understand?"

I was speechless. How wonderful. We aren't just poor, little humans who are trying desperately to become better, to finally create heaven on earth. We are not just looking enviously toward the angels and their realms, wondering why we don't live as they do. There is a greater plan. With our thoughts of love, hope and glory, we feed the world of angels. And, when they are fed, they have the power to help us become like them. What a wonderful circle!

Zarathustra continued to explain: "Some people believe that if one is feeling despair they should hold that thought constantly so the angels will know. What purpose would that serve? Nothing. It should be a celebration. It should be rapture. It should be enchantment. That is what we should constantly send to the angels as well as to the realm of the physical Gods, known as humanity."

So we have a responsibility for the angels, as well. Not only the angels for us. I had to think about that for awhile.

"Is Jao my guardian angel?"

"No, Jao was one of your angels who helped you grow."

I had noticed I hadn't heard him in awhile in my meditations. Instead I heard a thought coming into my mind that was not associated with a certain being or color. "He is probably somewhere else already," I said to myself.

I looked at Zarathustra, who smiled at me and nodded.

"My guardian angel, who has the highest image of me, does he have a name?"

"Yes, but all names follow tones. First they have a tone."

"Do I know that tone?"

"You know that tone. Of course, you know that tone."

In the way he shared this information, I knew he would not sing the tone to me. So it was my turn again. "Is it my 'Ohm'?" I had a special sound I hum before I meditate: my "Ohm."

"It is your 'Ohm,' but it is not limited to that. Your angel is your angel and relates to you within. I would not have

you feel that you can only connect vibrationally through a particular tone. Your vibration is your inner being. It is your goodness, your contribution, your offering of service. These are the things that place you and your angel in close proximity."

"Is there anything I can do to make this proximity even closer?"

"You are doing this. The big changes you went through in the last year have brought closer proximity. You are aware of it. You feel you live more and more in this realm. Don't you feel a peace within you that was unknown to you before?"

I nodded. I couldn't talk. I had a catch in my throat. Yes, that was true. In this last year many things had changed. Most important, I enjoyed my life now. The melancholy I used to feel had disappeared. And I knew why. It was because I now lived as my soul demanded. I didn't have to hide anymore. I was myself as I am. I came home to myself. Even if it were a challenge to my surroundings, I did what I felt was right. I had to swallow again.

"The only reason you have not seen the unfoldment is that you are continuously asked to be of service. You think certain deeds will be of service, and they are. Service is your life. When you understand sacrifice, you will see that part of your sacrifice has been to not actually see angels so that you can share this particular phase with others. That is your sacrifice. Do you understand?"

I started to cry. I was grateful that there was nothing I had done wrong or had neglected to do that prevented me from seeing my angels. I felt sadness about the sacrifice, while at the same time knowing everything was all right just the way it was. Understanding about this sacrifice was a relief to me. I understood and I grabbed for a tissue.

"But the sacrifice will have a reward," he continued. "You will be able to tell this to your fellow humans. They do not need to sacrifice, but they must be willing to trust that their angels are with them. When they do a good deed, they will see the angels. First they will feel the angel inside them. Then seeing becomes a reunion of sorts. And that is far more beautiful."

Zarathustra looked deep into my eyes. "That is very similar to what my woman (Jaqueline) has written in regard to the second coming. It will be felt at an individual level before it happens for the masses. That's why my brother Jesus brought the great light to her. That which supports the second coming and the great reunion on the physical level must first be felt as an inner reunion with the Christ."

Zarathustra stopped. "I did not come to this woman (Jacqueline) for her alone, but through her for all others. So also I come to answer your questions that you call 'linear-thinking.' You were drawn to be with me for your own awakening to God, which others may call salvation. All whom you touch will feel this vibration through you. When first I entered the body in this human plane, I said I came to teach the teachers. You are a fruit from that great tree. Give people your love unconditionally. Feed them as I have fed and shall feed you. Let them see through you the trueness, the reality that I am in God. Tell them that, when they read these words, some will have emotions of pure recognition and wish to know these feelings. Have them find a quiet moment, light a candle and then I will be with them. Not for the glory of my name as you know me, but for the Creator of the Light that vibrates within every cell of all life everywhere. I am in service to the great breath of life, and they will feel the love of God. I am that I am and so are all of you."

Zarathustra took a deep breath. "More will flow from this Light. More, as you know, will be taught. Tell them that the vibration between the angels and the gnomes and the fairy kingdom goes back in the history of their European culture. They live as giants among civilizations of smaller beings, who are gentle, playful and wise. Softness and gentleness flows from the beating of the heart of the people in your country (Germany). Ask them for the stories they may remember their mothers and their mothers' mothers told them. Let them reach into the treasure chest of memories and find the myths and legends and stories, and then ask questions. There will be a time you can ask me and I will give you yet another book for your country. I will weave this story for you, showing how it connects to all the myths and stories of this world. It will help people weave the great unification that is coming. By reaching back through time into mythic invention, they will see that life runs simultaneously through the time of their ancestors and peace rings through all dimensions of time and space."

Zarathustra leaned forward and held my face in his hands. I looked deep into his eyes that were always a little darker than Jacqueline's.

"And so be it."

Yes, and so it will be. I slowly said, "Thank you." My heart was full of the grace of his words. I felt I had known him forever in my heart. He released my face and widened his arms in a quiet blessing. After a couple of seconds, he lowered his arms, looked down at me and closed his eyes. I took one deep breath to absorb the vibration of Zarathustra deep inside me. Then his upper body fell lifelessly forward.

I picked up the glass of water sitting on the small table next to me. Whenever Jacqueline came back into her body, she usually started to cough and her throat was dry and in need of liquid. I softly said, "Ohm." Almost immediately Jacqueline's upper body jerked up with her usual cough. With her left hand she opened the top button of her silk tunic and at the same time breathed in deeply.

The feeling in the room was different now. Jacqueline's soul was back.

During my childhood I was, like so many of us, very sensitive and aware of the mood swings of those around me. As I grew into adolescence and adulthood, I noticed how painful these sensitivities were and I tried to get rid of them. I thought, "I just wish I had thicker skin," and I prayed I wouldn't have to suffer so much, or cry so much anymore. I hoped I would be strong and big. I also admired people who were cynics because, it seemed to me, they couldn't get hurt so easily. They use words as a weapon and shoot back sharpely. Somehow I was never able to develop thicker skin. I started to build walls around me to hide my defenseless, gentle soul. Until finally the walls broke down when my television career collapsed and revealed my tender, hurt soul again.

I have realized in recent years that my sensitivity is actually an enormous talent. Now I work with this talent. I let feelings happen and watch where they bring me. I don't follow them blindly as one is drawn into a vortex. Instead I watch my feelings as I would watch a movie and learn from them.

As I started to allow my sensitivity to show more, I also felt my body more. If my body were out of balance or sick, I knew

exactly where the center of disease was. This way, I didn't feel "bad" all over. I knew where something moved, where something cramped, what was soft and what felt unsure. I was more aware of mood swings in people and animals. I trained my body to become a sensitive receiver. No, that's not true: I rediscovered my body's natural talent to be a receiver.

I could feel when Zarathustra entered Jacqueline's body, even if my eyes were closed. His frequency connected with mine and my own frequency felt lighter. There was a light tickle on my arm. Often my hair stood up a little. Sometimes I had goosebumps. There was a pulsation in my body, a feeling of deep peace but also joyful excitement. When Zarathustra left Jacqueline, the transition was slower. His frequency remained in the room even after he had moved out of Jacqueline's body.

Jacqueline opened her eyes. "How are you?" she asked.

"Thank you very much. Thank you." I looked into her eyes and felt deep gratitude. It was exhausting for Jacqueline to share her body with someone else and I admired her commitment and generosity for offering such great love and service.

"I'm glad." She nodded at me. Jacqueline doesn't know when she comes back into her body what we have spoken about. After a while, the information that has remained in her field comes back to her, just as oil is absorbed into the skin. She lifted her head and said, "Ah, he spoke to you about fairies."

"Yes," I nodded as I massaged her legs, which had fallen asleep. I took some water from the bowl on my altar and touched the soles of her feet.

"Ah, that feels good."

I blew on her knee. Our breath holds our life force and I use this life force often. The deep love I carry in my heart moves through the breath to the other person and their cells react to that love.

"Thank you," Jacqueline said. Slowly she tried to stand up but she was still a little shaky. "What time is it?" she wanted to know.

"Noon."

"Oh wonderful. Then we have plenty of time to get to the airport."

Later, in the car, I had more questions. "Zarathustra spoke a lot about how we will get to our angel potential. How we can reach that. How important it is to think good thoughts, to increase our vibration. But what happens if someone is ill or even dies because of this illness? What influence does this have on their vibration and on their next life?"

"Well, often one has the feeling of not having done enough. Even people who take care of the terminally ill sometime experience that. Just think about Suzane."

Yes. My friend Suzane Piela had moved from Los Angeles to a tiny town in Wisconsin last year to take care of her mother who had cancer. She had done marketing for my company. When her mother became ill, she quit her job and moved to Wisconsin. Her father had died a couple of months before from cancer and, as she said good-bye with tears in her eyes, she told me, "I'm not ready yet to lose my mother, too."

Her parents were retired farmers and twice a month Suzane drove her mother to the nearest big city two hours away for chemotherapy. Suzane was very spiritual. She knew about the power of thought and prayer and about alternative healing methods. She knew about plants that can soften the aggressiveness of chemotherapy and plants that can boost the immune system.

She massaged her mother and laid her hands on her for healing. She talked with her about God, her soul and her choice to get healthy if she wished. Her mother was exhausted after a long farm life, raising seven children and taking care of her sick husband.

Suzane brought her mother to Los Angeles for a visit half a year after she had moved to Wisconsin. We three spoke about the choices we have. Suzane suggested to her mother that she spend the cold winter in a warmer climate, such as Hawaii. But her mother wanted to stay at her farm home in Wisconsin. Suzane gave her mother everything you could possibly give. She gave love and tenderness and she supported all her decisions, even when she did not agree with them. Still, when she saw that death was weakening her mother, she asked herself if she had overlooked something. Could she be doing more so her mother could live longer?

Jacqueline said, "Suzane did everything one could only possibly do. She showed her mother alternative healing methods, she talked about God and the choice each person has in life—yet her mother still died. Her mother decided to leave her body. That doesn't mean her soul did not enter a higher frequency. The healing process took place on the emotional, intellectual, and spiritual realms. Her mother accepted new wisdom and understood this knowledge as well. She found peace and healing and, through Suzane's help, learned to work through a lot of her experiences in this life. She died peacefully. When she passed away, she left her body differently than she would have if Suzane had not been with her. If someone dies with such peace, the soul reaches a different atmosphere than they would without the help of relatives or friends."

"But what can one do about the feelings of 'I missed something' or 'Did I do enough?' when someone dies—even if you tried to do as much as possible?" I asked.

"Many people were successfully healed, spiritually healed, yet they died anyway," Jacqueline explained. "Maybe they were exhausted from life. Maybe they wanted to be with God. I spoke recently with the renowned scientist, Dr. Valerie Hunt, an expert in the sensory field around the body. Often the sensory field is healed because it reflects our soul and spiritual wisdom. The soul as you know is not in the body. The soul is around the body. Each disease is first acknowledged in the sensory field. Dr. Hunt explains this process in her book *Infinite Mind*. Disease, as well as healing, always start in the sensory field. If the sensory field is healed, why does the person die anyway? 'Anyway' is not the right word. If the soul has reached a different level, then all the necessary healing has happened for that soul. Even if the person decided consciously or unconsciously that they wanted to die, the soul received healing. This is important to know."

"Don't we sometimes egotistically hope the body will be healed because we don't want to lose that person?"

"That may be the case. But the more clearly we know we are not just the body, the better we understand that healing is more than just fixing the body. This has to do with the great universal principle of cause and effect. Whatever you do has a reaction. Each act of tenderness and love offered to those who need it during sickness or at the time of passing, has a beneficial effect."

We arrived at the airport and I said good-bye and received a warm hug from Jacqueline. Again, I was thankful for all the wonderful people in my life. Each of us is a teacher and a student at the same time. We give what we know and receive what we need to learn. I waved from my car as I left the airport and entered the L.A. traffic.

On the way home I enjoyed the time of silence in my car and digested Jacqueline's wisdom. "What a comfort," I said to myself, "knowing that nothing is wasted." Even the littlest touch has a result. Of course, our soul receives the love and tenderness we give. Besides, wasn't it true that Suzane's mother had been exhausted? When they visited us, I asked Suzane's mom if she had decided she wanted to continue to live. There was a long pause before she answered. Her face seemed to get thinner as she thought about it. Her eyes fell even deeper into their sockets and her hands, that were touching each other on her lap, fell with palms open to the side.

"You know, I don't know Sabrina…." She searched for understanding in my glance. "Don't tell Suzane, but I'm really very tired."

My love for her spilled out like water overflowing from a cup. I tenderly took her white, fragile hand in mine. A hand that had cared for seven children, had cooked and washed; a hand that had planted flowers and gardens and that had washed her husband and fed him when he was sick. A hand that simply wanted to lie down, that wanted to be there without doing anything. I just held her hand in mine. I didn't even squeeze it because I knew the squeeze she would have to give in response would be too exhausting for her. She was tired. She wanted to go home to her true home. Four months later she passed away.

Chapter Sixteen

About a night alone in the forest and fairies who are also Angels, just a little smaller

I spent a lot of time alone in the next days, thinking about and enjoying the logic of Zarathustra's explanations. Before, when I knew nothing about frequencies, sensory fields, angels or the power of my thoughts, life seemed so unjust. People seemingly were born, out of the blue, into a particular family, without any sense of justice. Some had an easy life and others a hard life; some had good luck and others were unlucky; sometimes tragic struck and changed our lives completely. I felt helpless when others hurt me or when they were just "against me." Then I recognized that my soul was looking for a situation to grow by choosing my particular parents and surroundings. There was no one "against me." No one was trying to make my life "worse."

I have learned I always have a choice. In each situation in my life, there was a point at which I agreed to the choices that led me there. Sometimes my "No" was just not firm enough. Before, I never recognized the full spectrum of my choices. If I, for example, had an argument with my husband, I believed there was only one answer: I always wanted to win our argument. I didn't want to acknowledge his feelings in an argument. I just wanted to think about myself and how I felt and why I wanted it this way and not the other way. I didn't know that I had several options: I could be quiet; I could leave and calm down; I could meditate; I could laugh; I could hug him;

I could cry; I could ask; I could listen. I was not aware of this range of choices. I just reacted as I always did, according to my old behavior patterns. How much lighter my life had become. In place of my fears and sorrows was a deep understanding and trust in God and in my angels.

Zarathustra once said that fairies were angels for little people. That was a delightful thought.

I went to Breitenbush, Oregon to meet my Sacred Life Ministry friends for a spiritual weekend. I took my sleeping bag, which I hardly travel without, and enjoyed the two-hour drive from the Portland airport to Breitenbush. This area, which used to be a favorite meeting place for Native Americans, is surrounded by a beautiful ancient forest. Natural hot springs shoot out of the earth and create pools. Sacred pipes are smoked, dancing occurs and holy prayers are spoken. Many little, wooden cabins have been built there, as well as a larger building with a library, large dining room, meeting room and pyramid- shaped chapel.

I wanted to spend three nights. I had been told in a meditation to sleep outside, not in a cabin. The first two nights, I slept near the cabin. When I looked up, I could see the stars and moon through the pine trees. It was almost the full moon and I enjoyed all the tender sounds of the nearby forest. On the morning of the third day, I walked along a small path in the forest and to go to one of the hot springs.

All of a sudden I heard, "Stop" in my head. I wondered who had initiated that thought. "You will sleep in the forest tonight. All by yourself. We will guide you. Trust."

I still had no idea where this thought had come from. But I trusted that this was what I should do.

I spent the day in silence. I enjoyed the quiet even at mealtimes. I watched the leaves, how they danced and moved on the trees. I sat close to the riverbed and listened to the squirrels and birds. A day of silence calmed my sensory field.

All the input we allow to enter our minds, day after day, exhausts our sensory fields. This is not surprising, considering how much input we allow into our field—constant noise through the radio, TV, cars, telephones and so on. Once in a while I try to have a day of silence. During this day, I don't talk, read or listen to music from sunrise to sunset. I don't distract myself with anything. I stay with my thoughts, feelings and body. The first time I tried this, I was incredibly bored. I thought, "What should I do, for heaven's sake?" A restlessness moved through me, bringing up memories from my childhood, when I was told, "Don't sit around and be lazy and daydream. Do something!" Yes, I was told daydreaming was a waste of time. Today I know that daydreams help us create our reality. Time to daydream is equally as important as time for action.

I enjoyed the nature at Breitenbush. I listened to the river, which told me its story. I thought about India: "Be like a river." I watched a group of butterflies as they danced with each other. I lifted up a stone, closed my eyes and felt its corners, sharp ends and coolness.

Then it was time to get ready for my night in the forest. I had never slept in a forest alone. I wondered how I would feel. I changed into my warm clothes for the night, grabbed my sleeping bag and my flashlight and took one of my crystals with me.

I felt the cool wind on my head. Everything else was covered with warm fleece as I walked out of the cabin I shared with two other friends. I stood outside for a moment to feel in which direction I was being pulled. Straight ahead was what I sensed, so I walked in that direction. It was very dark, but a gentle light on the ground led me to the main building. Everything was quiet, as the others were having their dinner. As I stood at the entrance to the forest, I grabbed my flashlight and fumbled for the button to turn it on because the moonlight didn't shine through the thick crowns of the trees. I heard in my head: "Leave the light off. You do not have to awaken everybody."

"Okay," I said to myself. Then, all of a sudden, blasting in my head, I heard: "Are you crazy? You're going to sleep alone in the forest? Murder! Rape! You'll get yourself killed!"

My fear was trying to take over. No, I would not allow that to happen. I had to get rid of this fear and I knew how: only a prayer would get me out of this space. I dropped my sleeping bag and fell on my knees, with my hands touching the wet earth. I prayed: "Dear God, I am here because Spirit invited me to spend a night in this forest and I know that your love is always with me. I will only feed the thoughts that support this and elevate my vibration and my love."

My fear still tried to produce some scary words, but I kept repeating my prayer. I kept my focus as I felt the earth under my hands. I only thought of my love for God. Gradually I felt calmer and more relaxed. Finally I took a deep breath and congratulated myself: "Good job." I had controlled my thoughts instead of following an old fear.

I walked slowly into the forest. I followed my sensory field, sometimes gently bowing my head when I felt a branch come close. A minute later, I stopped again and sent out another prayer: "Dear forest, I am here because I have been invited from you and your world. Please, I don't want to have any crawling visitors in my sleeping bag and please I don't want to be woken up by scary noises. Let me sleep undisturbed. Except, of course, if there should be a wonderful vision waiting for me. In which case, please wake me up."

I waited a second and felt a gentle wind hugging me tenderly. This was the answer the forest was sending. I was understood. I kept walking on this little path that got narrower and narrower. Half an hour later, suddenly I had the feeling I had gone too far. I turned around and slowly walked back. My focus was inside, so I could stop when I felt guided to do so. One step further, another step; then I heard, "Stop." I tried to look around but it was too dark. I thought I could see a fallen tree trunk. I stretched out my arms and touched the dark mass. I felt moist, loose, dead bark. I had a strong feeling I should sleep next to this tree.

I put my sleeping bag down and, as I always did, crawled into my bag to see what I had to remove underneath. Sometimes it was a stone or a branch. I never slept on a mat because I liked the feeling of the ground under my back. I noticed nothing disturbing me as I lay down, which had never happened before. So I stayed in my bed. The trunk touched me as a mother would touch her child. I felt hugged and safe.

Finally everything was quiet. I wasn't moving around in the bag, the zipper was pulled up and I had made all the adjustments so I could lie down comfortably. I was curious how I would react to all the noises the forest makes at night. But there was nothing, except the sound of my breath. There was complete silence. I remembered my prayer in which I had asked for undisturbed sleep. What an accomplishment to keep the whole forest quiet! I felt honored and offered my thanks to the forest. The wind gently touched my face and I felt very comfortable, as I had felt when I was a little child in my mother's arms. For the first time I felt the earth was my mother. I felt it with all my senses.

Around 5 a.m. I woke up. I heard in my head, "Look to the left."

I could see the trunk that had hugged me all night, but I couldn't see anything else. "Look to the left," I heard again.

I sat up and stared to the left. Nothing. "Look next to the leaf."

There was a little leaf right on the trunk. "There is a magic wand."

A magic wand? Did I go crazy overnight? But, in fact I did see something very tiny with a funny green top. I pointed my index finger at it. "Is this it?"

"Yes, that is for your daughter."

Next to it was something green, mossy and soft. "That is also for your daughter," I heard. "We make clothes out of this. She will like it."

"Who are you?"

"We are fairies and little people. We live here."

"Can I see you?"

I heard giggling.

"No, no, that is enough for today."

"Thank you," I whispered toward the tree trunk. I wrapped the little presents carefully in a long leaf. What a night!

I was proud I had spent the night alone in the forest, and that I hadn't followed my old fears. Maybe I had become more selective about the information I let inside. I knew about the world's problems, about wars and violence, misunderstanding, aggression and hate. But was I aware of the influence all that had on me? Can we sincerely say that all the bad news, violent movies, negative books, cynical and judgmental thoughts and aggressive music don't have any influence on us?

A year earlier I had stopped watching news. I would watch again if it offered me a balanced view: good news and other news. Who says news always has to be bad? Now my source of information was the newspaper. I could more easily select the information I allowed to infiltrate my mind. Since I did not hear every day about murder and rape, I didn't think about it much anymore. I surrounded myself with things and people who elevated me. This felt good to me. This didn't mean I ignored the "other world" (I refused to call it the "real world" because we create our own reality). I helped wherever I could. I focused on the positive. There were enough people who focused on the negative. They didn't need me, as well.

I believed it was because of my selective news input that I was no longer afraid. I wanted to be someone who created peace and happiness, not someone who added to the fear and anger in the world. Peace begins within oneself. If we all loved ourselves and lived in peace and harmony, soon the whole world would be living in that peace. We all have to begin with ourselves.

My daughter Julia, for example, is not allowed to watch most movies. I always watch them first and then decide if they would have a positive influence on her. She doesn't need to see additional emotional conflict. She has enough to do to grow up.

Sometimes her friends at school asked me "Why can't Julia see that movie?" I explained, "I believe some movies make you happy and some make you afraid. I don't want Julia to be afraid, I want her to be happy. I don't want her to have bad dreams. That's the reason she's not allowed to see that movie."

I was surprised how well the children understood. I once read in the LA Times about a mother who was asked why she had brought her four-year-old to a movie that had a great deal of emotional conflict. She replied, "She wanted to see it for weeks. I just couldn't say no to her. There is so much peer pressure."

How sad she couldn't say, "No." No is often more difficult than yes. Of course, we are the ones responsible for our children's lives, not peer pressure.

Feeling comfortable has become a passion for me. I once thought I had to face the cruelty of the world. I believed people who were happy and content avoided facing the "reality" of life. But I completely overlooked the realities of my own life and how important it was for me to be happy.

That thought entered my mind a couple of years ago and I wanted to get rid of it immediately because I was afraid I'd have to change my whole outlook on the world. *I* would have to change. But what type of person would I become? A weirdo who always looked slightly drugged, who smiled at any catastrophe that came my way?

I remembered when in one of my meditations the angel Gabriela sent me a thought: "It is important to be smart. But wouldn't you rather be wise?"

What did it mean to be wise? Did it mean having more understanding and compassion; did it mean to support, to care and to love? The word "wise" sounds much softer than "smart." "Smart" sounds like a sword; "wise" like a gentle touch. Maybe intelligence coupled with love is how we should define wise.

Some time ago, my husband and I were invited to a dinner party by Monica and Niki. Monica is an art historian;

her husband, a director. They also invited a couple visiting from Germany. We sat around the fireplace and talked. Finally we ended up talking about the state of the nation. The men saw the world getting worse and worse. I tried to share my view: "But haven't we made major steps in the right direction? Isn't there more understanding now than, let's say, twenty years ago?"

I noticed by their looks that they thought I was naive. "But Sabrina, just look at the news!"

"But wouldn't it be better if we talked about what we would do to make the world better and not just stand there and shake our heads? We have to ask ourselves, 'What am I doing to make this world a better place?'"

At the end of the evening, I went home very quietly. There was something I didn't understand. I didn't want to try to convince people to change their opinions. That type of exchange wasn't satisfying for me anymore. I just wanted to share what I believed and accept other people's opinions.

I went to my altar and prayed. I asked my angels to explain how I could have better asserted myself. How could I have created a feeling of hope instead of conflict?

"Write down your vision of the world and send it to them. Write down how you see the future of humanity."

How wonderful. There it was. I didn't have to discuss endlessly until I had made each negative into a positive. If I shared my vision of the world, maybe I could inspire others to make that vision even better, even more beautiful, even more glorious. Then their daydreaming would also help make the world a better place. What a great idea!

I thanked my angels. I sat down at my computer. It was after midnight, but I didn't want to wait until tomorrow.

240

Chapter Seventeen

About how the world will look
when we can all see our Angels

We will recognize that everything is energy, energy that is constantly moving—each thought we think, each word we say and each deed we do. We will act differently, and in accordance with this energy.

The first thing to change will be the kind of food we allow into our bodies. We will only eat what is naturally grown and lovingly nurtured. We will know that animals who have lived in fear and pain all their lives are consumed in our bodies at the same frequency. Fear doesn't disappear because we deep-fry the meat. For this reason, we will start having our animals live in the most natural conditions possible, with love and honor. If it is time for us to kill them, there will be a ceremony and a prayer and we will take their sacrifice with gratitude and love. My girlfriend Samantha once met a shepherd who kissed his sheep on the forehead before he killed them. Unlike all the sheep who die screaming, his died in complete silence. There was no scream and no fear.

Everything we eat will be pure because we will have learned we can also get our energy from other sources. For this reason, we will eat less than we eat now. We will have learned that we can get the majority of our energies from the earth. We will walk barefoot so we can absorb the minerals through the soles of our feet into our body. We will often spend the night outside

to get energy from the light of the moon and the stars. We will live in a stress-free environment that does not take energy from us, but rather replenishes us.

We will live on the outskirts of big cities because we know that certain areas are more conducive to our receiving energy. The cities will be our centers of communication, but few people will decide to live there. We will live in apartments and houses that support our bodies and souls. We will have learned that we should only be surrounded by things that are enjoyable to us. We will have recognized and used the power of color, the power of smell, of plants and stones. Instead of square structures, our architecture will use round structures. We will understand that our energy flows more easily in a round environment.

We will have learned that we don't need clutter around us. We will no longer keep things we don't need anymore. Our closets will have only clothes we actually wear. Our homes will be filled with things we love. We will know our thoughts create our reality, so we will be careful about what we think. We will teach our children to honor the earth and all living things, and they will do so because we have provided a good example. Their reality will be joyful because they will have learned that humanity is gentle and good. Our children will see and feel what is gentle and good.

We will support each other because we realize that love and abundance are plentiful—and not like a cake that has limited pieces. We will realize that we feel much better when we live together, not against one another. We will all know we have lived before and will live again, and that each life exists for us to grow greater.

We will communicate telepathically because we won't have to hide our thoughts anymore. Our thoughts will be full of respect and love. No one will do what doesn't bring them joy. Work as we know it will have changed. Our hobbies will become our professions. Each minute we "work" will be joy for us. We will have learned that products made without love have an energy of boredom and desperation. We will not allow this energy to be anywhere near us because we will have become more sensitive. Since we no longer want these products, no one will produce them.

We will all have what we truly need and will be in balance with nature and our fellow humans. We will have greater understanding about our own past. We will understand that we filled our life with useless things because we felt lonely, insecure and desperate. We will not need status symbols anymore because our life will be filled with joy, productivity and peace. We will support each other and share our talents and products. Insurance companies, prisons and boring schools will not exist.

Because we have learned how important each newborn soul is, we will not have children simply because we need to fill our empty lives or need someone to love us unconditionally. We will have children because we want these newborn souls to continue to grow. We will understand this as service. We will know that God has given us free will and we can use this free will to choose how many children to bring into this world. We will control our bodies so well that our thoughts can be used for birth control. Because we will spend more time teaching our children, we will have fewer children than we have now.

We will have learned that our body, our soul and our mind can be raised by pure light and energy. We will have ceremonies during the different moon phases. We will know that it is easier to get rid of old things when the moon is

descending into a new moon. We will know it is easier to take new things on when it crests to a full moon. We will have long times of complete silence in our daily lives and we will be one with our higher self.

Disease will be a memory from the past. Because we will understand our bodies, and because we will live without any pollution, our bodies will have greater wellness. We will have learned that we can heal each other through our hands and our breath, with the help of the elements and, above all, with prayer. We will accept and gladly welcome the first symptoms of a disease as a little warning signal that our body has created to tell us something needs to be changed. Because we will understand these warning signals better before a full-blown disease develops, we will change accordingly. Instead of hospitals, we will have healing centers and doctors will be what they truly are: healers. They will work with other healers. These healing centers will be filled with love, music, incredible smells, touch, massages, exercise, talks, prayers, silence and dance. We will visit these centers to refresh our energies before we have a chance to become too exhausted.

We will not make love to each other because we are lonely or fearful. We will make love to each other because we honor each other. We will acknowledge that energy is exchanged through sexual intercourse, so we will exchange this energy only in love. And it will be sacred as well as fulfilling to us.

We will communicate with all living beings on this earth: the fairies, the angels, the little people and the kingdom of animals. We will see other more evolved beings because we also will be more evolved. We will all be able to be seen or not to be seen.

We will travel without planes because we will have learned that we can transport ourselves from one corner of the world to the next through mere thought. We will have gentle contact with our brothers and sisters from other planets and galaxies. These visitors will be able to visit us because we have raised our frequencies. We will know that everything we take in—each smell, each picture, each touch, each bite, each drink, each thought and each breath—has an effect on how we feel. So we will only hear, see, eat, drink, think, touch and breathe what supports our well-being and harmony. We will have moved the evolution of humankind one step forward. We will continue to grow because everything grows, and so do we.

It was wonderful to create such a vision. I would be delighted to hear yours. I wonder what will happen with our guardian angels. Of course, we will see them. Will we also reunite, and become one? What will happen if we become one vision? That is a very interesting thought.

I sent my vision by fax to Niki.

He called me back the next day. "My dear Sabrina, it sounds great. But unfortunately I can't believe this will ever happen."

"Some day the world will look this way. And the more each of us personally commits to it, the faster it's going to happen," I said.

I heard Niki laugh on the other end of the phone line. "Well, one thing I have to admit: your world definitely sounds better than the one I envisioned."

"You are more than welcome to join mine," I replied laughingly.

His last sentence stayed with me for a long time. We create our own reality. If money, beauty and health alone made us happy, everybody who had them would be happy. But we know that is not true. There is more.

What makes me happy? To be who I am. To know that I am loving and caring because I live in harmony with myself, God and the world. I am getting closer to that every day.

I have learned in the last few years how angels truly love us. They love us unconditionally. They understand and recognize in us the wish and the desire for peace and love. They love and support us. They heal us. They visit us, comfort us, and sometimes warn us. They wait for an open heart and an open mind to show us the way.

We can feel their love if we are looking for it. If we close our eyes and, in our hearts, ask for them to come, then we will feel them. We have the choice to open our window to the world of angels, even if it is just a tiny bit. Through the love of our angels and through our desire, this little opening gets bigger and bigger until the window is completely open. Someday even the window itself may completely disappear.

My deepest desire is that I could give you hope, trust and maybe even proof that the world of the angels is real. As real as the love we feel.

I was hoping that I would see my guardian angel before I finished this book. Well, I haven't seen him yet. But that hasn't stopped me. Quite the contrary. I focus even more on what I do know of him. I know that he is there. I feel him and I sometimes hear him and I know that I am loved endlessly.

I know and trust that someday I will see him. When I will see him depends on me. It is my choice to control my thoughts, to understand my fellow humans and to love them.

With this choice, I will reach my goal to become as close to my angel as possible.

"The way is the goal," some smart human once said. My way has brought me closer to my goal of finding peace within myself.

Four years ago, I was ninety-five percent unhappy, restless, lonely, upset, angry and sad. Today I am ninety-five percent happy, calm, relaxed and joyful. The rest of the five percent I am sure I will get. To feel complete happiness and be able to share it is the vision I have for myself. And, believe me: if I can do it, so can you!

I am going to close my eyes now. I will search for the sound. Wasn't it the sound that would bring my guardian angel to me?

God bless you.

248

Epilogue

*"But Sabrina, by all means, shouldn't you rethink your
book? Shouldn't you be a little bit more decent about all
your experiences. God and angels should be a private
matter, you shouldn't talk in public about it. Don't you
think you are missing humility and modesty?"*

About three years ago, I received a Christmas card with a
quote from President Nelson Mandela's inauguration speech.
It said:

*Our deepest fear is not that we are inadequate.
Our deepest fear is that we are powerful beyond measure.
It is our light, not our darkness, that most frightens us.
We ask ourselves, who am I to be brilliant, gorgeous,
talented and fabulous?
Actually, who are you not to be?
You are a child of God.
Your playing small doesn't serve the world.
There's nothing enlightened about shrinking.
so that other people won't feel insecure around us.
We were born to make manifest
the glory of God that is within us.
It's not just some of us; it's in everyone.
And as we let our own light shine,
we unconsciously give other people permission
to do the same.*

I carry this quote in my purse. I clearly remember how impressed I was when I read it for the first time. Today, when I read it, I am still touched by the depth.

Yes, we were taught to be modest—modest to the verge of self-denial. "Who am *I* to think I am special?"—"No, there is nothing special about me."—"Everybody can do what I can do."—"No, I am not pretty, just look at my big behind."

We belittle ourselves, so nobody gets jealous. We are afraid to be proud of ourselves—after all, being proud lies so near to being vain. However, with our attempt not to be vain, we throw out the baby with the bath water: We do not allow us to love ourselves.

Years ago during an interview, I was asked if I loved myself. I answered: "I have gotten used to myself." As if I were an infectious virus! I felt very self-conscious about what other people might have thought of me had I said: "Yes, I love myself." It sounded so selfish, arrogant, self-centered, snobbish (you may add to this list …).

We have to learn to love ourselves. For if we do not love ourselves, we cannot love other people. We cannot give what we don't have. If there is anything we do not like about ourselves, we—and we alone—have the power to change it. After all, God gave us our free will. If our light doesn't shine bright enough, we can clean that lamp. It is time, I believe, to show our light. Two thousand years ago, Jesus told us in the Sermon of the Mount: *"You are the light of the world. A city built on a hill cannot be hid. No one after lighting a lamp puts it under the bushel basket, but on the lampstand, and it gives light to all in the house. In the same way, let your light shine before others, so that they may see your good works and give glory to your Father in heaven."* (Matthew 5.14-5.16)

Don't we often shout out the negative things the loudest? Let us start to praise the good things! I thank God and my angels every morning for the blessing and the gift that I can share joy and inspiration with others. Let the light shine in all of us, so the world may be the paradise it was promised to be. And each light that is shining a little bit brighter in one of us will help to expel the darkness.

Once, Zarathustra said: "When someone asks you where you are from tell them you come from where the light is produced."

May we all remember this.

With light and love and God's blessings

Sabrina Fox

252

Native American Wisdom

My love of the world of angels is similar to my love of nature. There is a balance. We are like trees: if you want to stand tall, you need deep roots. Otherwise you will fall.

Our spirituality has to show us a gentle way to live with Mother Earth. There are many ways to do it. Some people like to hike. Some have a little garden. Some have plants on their balcony. Some are interested in shamanism and Celtic rituals. Others, like me, are interested in Native American wisdom. Everything is God, it is just a different way of expression.

To believe in angels and to smoke respectfully the sacred pipe at the same time is not a contradiction, as it may seem. I will give you the opportunity to understand a little better how I became a pipe carrier.

In 1994, I experienced a pipe ceremony for the first time. My friend Jacqueline Snyder, who has half-Cherokee and half-white blood, invited us to join her around a sacred fire at the end of a workshop. Her Spirit name is Eagle Speaks Woman.

My only connection to Native Americans was through Jacqueline. When I was a little girl, I always liked Indians in the movies better than the whites. I felt they were not handled fairly. Their land and culture were taken away from them in the name of religion, and in the name of greed and social gain. Their culture was almost destroyed. They were

called savages and wild men only because we, the Europeans, didn't understand their culture. They honored Mother Earth and the Great Spirit.

The peace pipe, as it was called by the white man, is a ceremonial pipe. Because the pipe was only shared with the white man in peace ceremonies, he didn't understand that it was smoked much more often, and for many reasons. The pipe made prayers visible. The smoke carried those prayers up to the Great Spirit.

With wide eyes, I watched Eagle Speaks Woman open her leather pipe bag and take out special objects. First there was an abalone shell with sage, then a fan made out of feathers. After that, she took out two packages—one long and thin, wrapped in a red cloth; the other, rather square, also wrapped in a red cloth—as well as different stones and shells, a bag for the tobacco and a turtle rattle.

She opened the two red cloths, revealing the pipe bowl and pipe stem. Her pipe was almost white, beautifully carved and decorated with feathers. The pipe bowl was shaped in the head of an eagle. "The parts of the pipe are always handled separately. The pipe bowl represents the female; the stem, the male. To begin a pipe ceremony, you connect them both, waking up the pipe so it becomes an instrument of prayer," explained Eagle Speaks Woman.

Eagle Speaks Woman was not an Indian name, but rather a Spirit name; that is, the name to which our soul listens. Native Americans honor nature in the form of the "four-legged ones," the "winged ones" and the "two-legged" ones. They are all relatives, whose job it is to live in harmony with one another. The wind is your brother; the earth, your mother. When Native Americans killed an animal, it was killed in ceremony. A pipe was

smoked beforehand, and they danced and prayed to the spirit of the animal to participate. Depending on the tribe, different rituals honored the soul of the animal who was sacrificing itself for its two-legged relatives. Every part of the animal was used: the skin, the meat, the bones, the hair; nothing was left. Back then, animals were only hunted when there was a need. Later, however, buffalo were killed for their fur and the rest of the body was left to rot.

I was surprised by the pipe ceremony. As a German, it was foreign to me, but I was fascinated. A pipe ceremony takes about an hour or more and has several rules. First sage and sweet grass are burned to cleanse the participants and the pipe. Then the pipe is filled with tobacco. The style in which the ceremony is conducted depends on the person and the tribe, but the essence is always the same. You focus on the prayer and make it visible. The smoke of the pipe is blown in all directions: first up to the Great Spirit and down to Mother Earth, then in the four directions, then to the fire that represents life and finally to oneself. There is no wrong way to smoke a pipe, as long as it is treated with respect and love. The pipe is for Native Americans what the rosary is for the Christian world.

At the end of the ceremony, I watched Eagle Speaks Woman close her eyes and press the stem of the pipe vertically on her forehead. After a while, she opened her eyes and nodded to a man sitting in front of her. He lifted his eyebrows in question. Eagle Speaks Woman motioned for him to come closer to her. He sat down in front of her with his legs crossed. Eagle Speaks Woman relit the pipe. She put the mouthpiece against the man's heart

and blew the smoke into his heart. Then she closed her eyes.

"What could that mean?" I asked myself. I wondered how it would feel to have smoke blown into your heart.

"Your name is Buffalo Heart. The buffalo is the only animal who faces the storm. All other animals turn around and show their back. You have the heart of a buffalo. You are strong in your love and you face each challenge. May you carry this name in honor," explained Eagle Speaks Woman.

I heard crying and was surprised to see it came from this bear of a man who was about forty years old. This name must have meant something for him. I was happy for him. Eagle Speaks Woman gave him a piece of fur. "This is from my buffalo."

The man gently took the fur in his hand and bowed his head. Eagle Speaks Woman nodded to him and he stood up.

Some months later I was again the guest at a pipe ceremony. This time I was given my own name. "Your name is Soaring White Eagle and your Spirit is the Light."

I had previously seen a white eagle in my meditations. I asked White Star Woman, Sharon Walker, a pipe carrier and expert in sacred pipes, what my name meant.

She said, "An eagle sees very wide and has good perception. He sees clearly and this clarity and great perception are its gifts. This is the medicine this name has given you. But you have also earned this name with your life so far."

Jacqueline added later, "The eagle is also the messenger of God. He is a sacred bird who brings wisdom to humanity."

"What does it mean that my Spirit is the Light?"

White Star woman answered, "Your Spirit is the Light. The Light is God and that is why you feel guided by God."

I was deeply grateful for this eagle. I felt immediately comfortable with this name. If it were up to me, I would never have been called Sabrina again. I started to sign my Spirit name when I wrote letters to close friends.

When a child is given a Spirit name, that name often changes over the years until the child becomes an adult. On my next birthday I was thirty-six. My friend Suzane brought me a white feather, my most precious gift. I also wanted to have a pipe but I had to wait. One is ready to receive a pipe only after one has had a vision of it. Visions do not come on demand; they come when you are ready. I had to wait patiently for my vision.

In the meantime, I understood better what these names meant. There are not only the name and the Spirit, but also the clan and the warrior. First there is the name and then the Spirit comes; then the clan and the warrior. The warrior has nothing to do with war; it has to do with courageousness. A warrior is someone who is courageous, who handles life with honor. Courageousness and honor are most challenged in an actual war, which is why it is called "warrior."

Since I received the name Soaring White Eagle, I have earned the qualities of the eagle and accepted them. I have the gifts of the eagle in my life. Much information comes through a name. Different animals have different talents. When an animal becomes your medicine, you receive its talents. A buffalo, for example, faces adversities. A turtle stands for wisdom, a bear for strength and a deer for grace.

Some months later, I noticed a wolf come into my meditations. I found myself in a forest and suddenly saw a wolf at my right side. He stared at me and started to run ahead of me. I knew I should follow him. My eagle was flying above me. I felt as if we were running all day until, at last, we reached a mountain. On top of this mountain was a tree. The eagle rested on a branch at the top of the tree, while the wolf stood beside the tree and invited me to sit next to him. I leaned against the tree and my vision ended.

When we were at Breitenbush, I was not surprised when I was told my clan. We sat in a ceremony with five other pipe carriers and, again, I was asked to come forward. Smoke was blown into my heart, and I was told that the wolf was my clan. I immediately started to cry. I had an irresistible urge to sing like a wolf.

"You can't do that," I told myself quickly.

"Why not?"

Tears ran down my cheeks as I sang the "Song of the Wolf." Afterward I was exhausted. I felt as if I had just climbed a mountain.

"Let me explain the medicine of the wolf clan," said White Star Woman. "The clan represents the family. You belong to the wolf family. The wolf brings the gift of humbleness. A wolf takes care of his family. He always makes sure that everyone else eats first, before he takes something. A wolf often goes off alone to ponder. He comes back when he knows the answers to his questions."

As I spent time thinking about this, I recognized its truth. I always made sure others were taken care of first. I often went off alone to think about things. I also felt this humbleness in me. Thank you.

I was still waiting for my pipe vision. I watched with envy as others handled their pipes. A couple of months later, I finally saw my pipe. In one of my meditations, I was staring into the flame of a candle and there it was. I saw a gray-headed man bring my pipe. The pipe stem had a wave in it and the head was a wolf with an eagle on top of it.

I didn't know the gray-haired man. "Funny," I said to

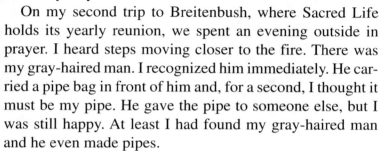

myself. "I hope I meet him soon." I trusted this man would come my way because visions don't come from nowhere.

On my second trip to Breitenbush, where Sacred Life holds its yearly reunion, we spent an evening outside in prayer. I heard steps moving closer to the fire. There was my gray-haired man. I recognized him immediately. He carried a pipe bag in front of him and, for a second, I thought it must be my pipe. He gave the pipe to someone else, but I was still happy. At least I had found my gray-haired man and he even made pipes.

The next day I went to see him. His name was Neil. I gave him some tobacco, the traditional gift to honor a person. Tobacco comes from Mother Earth, so the person to whom I give tobacco receives a blessing. I asked him to pray with me and to see if he would have a vision of my pipe. We sat around the pipe and Neil closed his eyes. Ten minutes later, he opened his eyes and said, "You will have a man pipe, a large pipe. It has a wave in the stem and the head is a wolf with an eagle."

I was ecstatically happy. How miraculously Spirit works.

That night I was given my warrior name: Rainbow Warrior. As I said, warrior has nothing to do with war. A warrior takes care of his family with his talents and his love and, in my case, the rainbow. The rainbow includes all the colors of light. Since my Spirit is the Light, that also made sense. I flew back and forth between Los Angeles and Germany, forming a rainbow bridge between the different cultures. I, as Rainbow Warrior, brought people together.

The next months I spent waiting. Such a pipe is not made between Wednesday and Thursday. The right stone needed to be found. The right wood. The moon must be right. Sometimes the wood must rest before it is handled.

Everything needed time. Finally, finally, it was time for me. I had to go to Seattle, where Neil lived, to pick up my pipe. Since I was in Munich with my daughter Julia, instead of going directly back to L.A., I decided to make a stopover in Seattle.

On my second-to-last day in Munich, I invited my sisters and some of my girlfriends to have dinner at my mother's house, where I was staying. Whenever I was in Germany, I smoked. I used to smoke before I moved to L.A. and in Germany, somehow, this old habit caught up with me. We were in the kitchen, laughing, drinking wine, smoking and having a wonderful time. I didn't go to bed until almost three o'clock. I closed my eyes for meditation. During the last month, in my meditations next to my angel Euphenia, I had often seen an old Indian chief by a fire. His name was White Wolf. He was gentle, but also very stern with me. This time I was completely surprised by his greeting.

"What, in heaven's sake, do you think you're doing?" he screamed at me.

I had barely closed my eyes. He stood behind the fire and his eyes were fierce, full of anger. I had no idea why he was so angry with me. I asked in surprise, "Why? What did I do?"

"You used the smoke as if it were nothing!" he yelled at me.

"Oh, you must mean my cigarettes. But—"

I didn't have a chance to explain myself. "You want to be a pipe carrier and you don't have respect for smoke?"

I decided to apologize. An explanation wouldn't work. I had heard of pipes that had broken after their first use because the pipe carrier, for example, had drunk alcohol before the ceremony. I had waited for my pipe too long to lose it because of a stupid habit.

"From now on, you will not smoke," he ordered me. When I say he ordered me, I mean order. I had no choice. Either I stopped smoking or there would be no pipe. That was that. Stupidly enough, I couldn't stop myself from asking for how long this would be. I realized immediately that was a huge mistake. "Because you have asked, you will also stop drinking at the same time. No cigarettes and no alcohol for a year."

I stop asking questions. Who knows what he would forbid me next.

Later I told my husband on the phone that I had stopped smoking.

"What do you mean you stopped smoking?" he said in disbelief.

I told him about my meditation.

"I'm not sure I understand that correctly. All these years, I asked you to stop smoking without any effect whatsoever. And now an old Indian in your head tells you to stop and you stop?"

I smiled. "Yes," I answered with a grin. "You understood correctly."

"Ah-ha. Well, I guess if it works, I'm okay with your old Indian."

It worked. I haven't drunk or smoked in almost three years.

I flew to Seattle and picked up my pipe. Julia sat next to me by the fire as Neil opened the pipe. It was heavy and long—a little bit too long. Pipes have to be moved in different directions and I had to stretch out my arm extremely far not to hit myself over the head every time. The mouth piece

was also too long. First I thought I needed to give it back to Neil to make it shorter, but then White Wolf came and said, "The pipe will only be yours when you work with it."

I understood. I flew home and bought myself some wood-carving tools. I had never carved wood. I prayed that I be shown what to do. I took the pipe on my lap and asked Spirit how I should proceed.

"Wet the wood before you work on it," I heard in my head

That's what I did. I was surprised how easy it was to carve the pipe. I had great fun with it. With each movement, the pipe became mine. Before it had been an art object, but now it became a prayer object.

I have had my pipe for almost four years now. It is my holy object, like my rosary, crystal cross, small Buddha statue, feathers and stones.

On my last birthday, my husband Richard bought me a teepee. It was a glorious day when we erected it. With my husband by my side, I invited my six spiritual sisters, all pipe carriers, for the ceremony. On each of the wooden poles that extend out of the top of the teepee, are prayer tags. Prayer tags are little pieces of cloth that are knotted together with tobacco inside. You say a prayer into the tobacco before you wrap it into the strip of cloth and hang it over the tee-pee. Then Brother Wind can carry the prayer out into the world. We all prayed for peace and understanding for each other and for the world. Each time I felt the wind, I knew our prayers were carried further.

I wanted to share a little bit of the information I have acquired over the years about the culture and wisdom of Native Americans. There are several books available, written by Native Americans, that provide detailed knowledge about this topic. You also can make a prayer tag. Take a piece of cloth, white or red, one inch by ten inches, and put some tobacco in your left hand. Close your eyes and say your prayer into it. First you pray for someone else and then for yourself. Afterward put the tobacco into the cloth, and fold the cloth over and tie the cloth into a knot. There are different ways to send your prayer to the Great Spirit. You can either burn the prayer tag or hang it on the bough of a tree. If you like, please try it. You will enjoy it. God bless you.

263

264

Meditations and Prayers

I wish to share with you some of my favorite meditations. They are easy. If you would rather have a taped version of the meditations, you can order it from My Angel and I.

Find yourself a very comfortable and quiet space. You can lie down if you prefer. Don't cross your legs. Make sure you are not disturbed and there is no noise. Take at least twenty minutes. If you can be outside in nature, lie flat on the earth or sit against a tree. These meditations also work well in the bathtub.

Let me say a few words about prayers. Prayer is your conversation with God, in which you express your desires. I am often asked how I know my angels are really talking to me and that I am not just imagining it. It is desire that makes the difference. If you sit in the car and move the gear stick into drive, you know you will go forward and not backward.

When I talk to my angels, I pray first. With this prayer, I tell God what I want. For example, "Dear God, dear angels. I thank you for your love and caring and I ask to receive wisdom about these questions." My desire to drive in first gear—that is, to make contact with my angels—is what carries me forward.

The only thing you have to do is trust. You learn trust when you do what you have been told and, the more you do this and find what you have been told is true, the more you will trust. I now trust all the information I have received from the angels because they have proven it to me over and over again.

Angels speak mostly in our thoughts. In rare cases, the heavens open up and God, or the guardian angels, appear in front of us with all their glitter and glory and speak to us. Guardian angels use our minds and intuition to make contact with us. It is the same when I receive a fax. It arrives in my fax machine; it is on my paper and my ink is on it. But the fax comes from someone else. How do I know? Because my fax machine is constantly turned on to receive faxes from someone wanting to fax me. Likewise, with angels, my inner fax machine is open, through my prayer, and I wait for their message. I know these messages come from the angels in the same way I know my paper faxes come from someone else.

The more you practice communicating with the angels, the more you achieve mastery with it. Someone once explained to me how our connection with God and our angels functions. "If you have a lamp at home and you turn it on but it doesn't work, you don't think there is no energy left in the world. You first check if the light bulb has burned out or if the cord has been plugged in. With us and God, it's the same thing. God is like electricity coming out of the socket. It is always there. We are the lamp and it depends on us whether we are "plugged in" or "turned on."

I have taken Zarathustra's advice and integrated more music into my prayers. Now, most of them are sung. Through my voice, my soul connects with God and worships him. I try to sing and worship for one hour every day to stay healthy and keep my vibrations high.

Pink Light
How To Feel Your Guardian Angel

Take some deep breaths in and out. Listen for awhile to the sound of your breath. Even if you feel you are finished, continue for at least five more minutes.

Then say your prayer. It can be as simple as, "I want to feel my guardian angel." Whatever you want, just say it. Sing.

Then imagine a soft, pink light around your heart. Focus on this light. Your guardian angel will send a feeling to you through this light. Scan your body and don't forget that the more you practice, the more you will feel your guardian angel. The peace and happiness that come to you are the feelings your guardian angel has sent.

- ⊛ Close your eyes.
- ⊛ Listen to your breath.
- ⊛ Say your prayer.
- ⊛ Sing.
- ⊛ Imagine pink, colored light around your heart.
- ⊛ Feel your guardian angel.
- ⊛ Give thanks.

How To See Your Guardian Angel In Your Inner Eye

Make yourself comfortable in a quiet environment. This meditation takes twenty minutes.

Listen to your breath. Say a prayer in which you voice your desires, using your own words to make your prayer personal. Sing. Then imagine that you are in a lovely meadow where you can watch nature around you. Watch the trees, listen to the sounds and sense the smells. Just relax in this meadow.

Look up and you will see a rainbow. Lie down in the meadow and let the colors of the rainbow come into your body. Trust that each color knows where to go. In this way, your healing process will be automatic.

When you feel complete, stand up and find a ladder that goes to the top of the rainbow. The ladder is there. Your guardian angel will be waiting for you at the top of the ladder. You can ask your guardian angel any questions you wish to know. Trust that you do not have to search for the answers. The answers will come to you. Sometimes this process is like playing a game of charades. Keep asking until you find a satisfactory answer. If you are the type of person who is visual, ask your guardian angel to send a visualization.

At the end of the meditation, thank your guardian angel knowing that you can always find him or her again at the top of the rainbow.

- Close your eyes.
- Listen to your breath.
- Say your prayer.
- Sing.
- Imagine a meadow with the rainbow above.
- Climb up the ladder towards your guardian angel.
- Ask your question.
- Give thanks.

Looking For Answers

Close your eyes and imagine that you are leaving your body. Watch yourself from above. Go higher and higher until you can see your surroundings and your house. Go even higher until you see the area where you live. Keep going higher until the whole earth is in your view.

Now say your personal prayer and ask your question— any question. Wait for an answer. The answer will come by itself. You don't have to look for it, because the answer is looking for you. Just wait and remember that the answer will always come. Don't forget to give your thanks at the end.

Deep Relaxation

If you are nervous, angry or can't sleep and a thousand thoughts come into your head and you are completely restless, this meditation will help you:

Listen to your breath. Focus on how you breathe in and how your breathe out.

That is all.

Meditation To Come Out of Sadness

Sing! You cannot cry and sing at the same time.

Meditation To Enter the Realm of Positive Thinking

Choose a prayer. Personally, I prefer the Lord's Prayer. Pronounce every single word deliberately. This will align you with God. Repeat it as often as you need to.

It is especially effective at the first signs of anger, despair and loneliness.

My Favorite Way to Pray

I am on my knees in front of a candle. I listen to my melody deep inside of me. First, I only hum, then I sing the melody aloud as my worship to God. By listening to my own melody, I connect with my origin, which is GOD.

Contact Information

If you would like to contact Sabrina Fox directly or are interested in ordering one of her meditation tapes please write to:

My Angel and I, Inc.
9460 Wilshire Blvd.
Suite 600
Beverly Hills, CA. 90212
USA
Fax: +1-310-285-0080

Sabrina Fox